The Tyndale New Testament Commentaries

General Editor: PROFESSOR R. V. G. TASKER, M.A., D.D.

D1140373

THE EPISTLE OF PAUL
TO THE GALATIANS

THE EPISTLE OF PAUL

TO THE

GALATIANS

AN INTRODUCTION AND COMMENTARY

by

R. A. COLE, M.TH., PH.D.

Tutor, St. Peter's Hall, Singapore

LONDON

THE TYNDALE PRESS

Thirty-nine . Bedford Square . W.C.1

© The Tyndale Press
First Edition—June 1965
Reprinted—August 1969

STANDARD BOOK NUMBERS:

CASEBOUND EDITION 85111 616 7
INTERNATIONAL EDITION 85111 817 8

Made and printed in England by
STAPLES PRINTERS LIMITED
at their Rochester, Kent, establishment

GENERAL PREFACE

ALL who are interested in the teaching and study of the New Testament today cannot fail to be concerned with the lack of commentaries which avoid the extremes of being unduly technical or unhelpfully brief. It is the hope of the editor and publishers that this present series will do something towards the supply of this deficiency. Their aim is to place in the hands of students and serious readers of the New Testament, at a moderate cost, commentaries by a number of scholars who, while they are free to make their own individual contributions, are united in a common desire to promote a truly biblical theology.

The commentaries are primarily exegetical and only secondarily homiletic, though it is hoped that both student and preacher will find them informative and suggestive. Critical questions are fully considered in introductory sections, and also, at the author's discretion, in additional notes.

The commentaries are based on the Authorized (King James) Version, partly because this is the version which most Bible readers possess, and partly because it is easier for commentators, working on this foundation, to show why, on textual and linguistic grounds, the later versions are so often to be preferred. No one translation is regarded as infallible, and no single Greek manuscript or group of manuscripts is regarded as always right! Greek words are transliterated to help those unfamiliar with the language, and to save those who do know Greek the trouble of discovering what word is being discussed.

There are many signs today of a renewed interest in what the Bible has to say and of a more general desire to understand its meaning as fully and clearly as possible. It is the hope of all those concerned with this series that God will graciously use what they have written to further this end.

R. V. G. TASKER.

CONTENTS

CHIEF ABBREVIATIONS

Abbott-Smith	*A Manual Greek Lexicon of the New Testament* by G. Abbott-Smith, 3rd edition, 1937.
Arndt-Gingrich	*A Greek-English Lexicon of the New Testament* edited by W. F. Arndt and F. W. Gingrich, 1957.
AV	English Authorized Version (King James), 1611.
Bruce	*The Book of Acts* by F. F. Bruce, 1962.
Burton	*The Epistle to the Galatians* by E. de W. Burton, 1921.
Daube	*The New Testament and Rabbinic Judaism* by D. Daube, 1956.
Davies	*Paul and Rabbinic Judaism* by W. D. Davies, 1955.
Duncan	*The Epistle to the Galatians* by G. S. Duncan, 1934.
Ellis	*Paul's Use of the Old Testament* by E. E. Ellis, 1957.
Guthrie	*New Testament Introduction: The Pauline Epistles* by D. Guthrie, 1961.
Jennings	*Lexicon to the Syriac New Testament* by W. Jennings, 1926.
Judge	*The Social Pattern of the Christian Groups in the First Century* by E. A. Judge, 1960.
Lightfoot	*The Epistle to the Galatians* by J. B. Lightfoot, 1900.
LXX	Septuagint (pre-Christian Greek version of the Old Testament).
Metzinger	*Introductio Specialis in Novum Testamentum* by A. Metzinger, 1956.
Moffatt	*An Introduction to the Literature of the New Testament* by J. Moffatt, 2nd edition, 1912.
	A New Translation of the Bible by J. Moffatt, 1926.
Munck	*Paul and the Salvation of Mankind* by J. Munck, 1959.
NEB	New English Bible: New Testament, 1961.

9

Robert et Feuillet	*Introduction à la Bible* by A. Robert and A. Feuillet, 1959.
Ropes	*The Singular Problem of the Epistle to the Galatians* by J. H. Ropes (Harvard Theological Studies), 1929.
RSV	American Revised Standard Version, 1946–52.
RV	English Revised Version, 1881.
Schoeps	*Paul; the Theology of the Apostle in the Light of Jewish Religious History* by H. J. Schoeps, 1961.
Wikenhauser	*New Testament Introduction* by A. Wikenhauser, 1958.

AUTHOR'S PREFACE

THE Epistle to the Galatians is spiritual dynamite, and it is therefore almost impossible to handle it without explosions. It has often been so in the history of the Church. The great spiritual awakening of Martin Luther came as he expounded and studied this Epistle, while it was a sermon on Galatians that brought peace of heart to John Wesley. Small wonder that both of these men dearly loved the book; it spoke directly from Paul's experience to their own. But this letter is not one with a message simply for those of centuries earlier than ours, nor is it an Epistle that can be read in comfortable detachment without personal involvement. At every point it challenges our present-day shallow, easy acceptances and provokes our opposition. It was a controversial letter; and it is vain to expect any commentator, however humble, to avoid controversy when expounding it—especially when the issues are just as alive today. The only danger is that we may try to use God's Word as a 'big stick' wherewith to belabour our theological opponents instead of allowing the exegesis to search our own hearts and condemn our own cherished presuppositions.

What, then, is the Epistle to the Galatians? It is a statement of Paul's gospel, which is also that of the Church universal. It is an *apologia pro vita sua* by the prince of apostles. So far, so good; but already we may be on dangerous ground. For Paul was a man whose 'orders' were not accepted by many of his fellow-countrymen. His claim to apostleship they regarded as unwarranted. More; in its refusal to allow salvation to depend on anything save the work done for helpless man by God almighty, and enjoyed by a faith which is itself the gift of God, it is a cry for Christian freedom. True, this condemns those who make salvation depend on forms and ceremonies as well as on faith in Christ (for the crime of the Judaizers was not that they substituted something for Christ's work, but that

11

they tried to add something to it). But it equally condemns those earnest Christians who subconsciously make salvation depend, not only on faith in Christ, but also on the observance of negative moral laws ('There are three things I will not do . . . ', in the words of the old negro spiritual). Which of us can throw the first stone?

Furthermore, at the risk of being accused of an anachronism, it could be said that Galatians is a passionate appeal for Inter-Communion. The table-fellowship for which Paul fought at Antioch was certainly not restricted to the Lord's Table, but it is hard to see how it could have failed to include it. On a matter like this, it is painfully easy to allow our own pet theological or ecclesiastical prejudices to blind our eyes; but Paul's reaction is obvious. He cannot conceive the possibility of two groups of Christians in one place who refuse to eat with each other because of theological scruples (for we wrong the Judaizers if we fail to realize that, whatever we may think about the 'play-acting' of Peter and Barnabas, this was a real theological scruple with them).

Again, there seems to be here a recognition that it is possible for the Church of God to be one without being uniform in custom, habit, or sphere. Paul never seems to have com-pelled the Gentile churches to act like Jews; indeed, this is precisely the charge that he brings against the erring Peter. Now those of us with a 'Reformed' background find this congenial and easy to understand. But it remains equally true that he does not expect Jewish churches to act like Gen-tile believers; he never says that it is wrong for them to be circumcised, or to keep the law, or to observe the festivals. All he insists is that these things have nothing to do with the gift of salvation. Not only so, but there is also a glad recog-nition of differences of sphere appointed by God: Paul is to go to the Gentiles; James and the rest are to work among the Jews.

This involves full mutual recognition, which is symbolized, not by any supplemental ordination, but by the offering of the 'right hand of fellowship'. Mutual trust, mutual acceptance, mutual recognition: was this a slender platform on which to work? Yet it was on such a basis that the whole Mediterranean basin was won for Christ.

These are hard sayings for all of us; and who can hear them? Yet, if this is indeed the message of Galatians for today, surely we neglect it at our peril.

R.A.C.

INTRODUCTION

AT the outset any study of the letter to the Galatians must at least try to answer three questions. First, To whom was the Epistle written? Second, At what time was it written? Third, Why was it written? All of these outwardly simple questions are in fact extremely complex; and to some extent the answer that we give to the first will determine our answers to the other two. In spite of all the advances in New Testament scholarship over the past decades, it is probable that we are no nearer to a final answer to these problems than our fathers were. All that we can do in a work of this size is to outline the main positions held, and the reasons for holding them, with mention of a personal preference for one or other of the contending views. But where certainty is virtually impossible it is wise to keep an open mind. Perhaps in years to come some chance archaeological or literary discovery may give us the necessary clue. Meanwhile, the only verdict possible is that allowed by old Scots law, 'not proven'; and it would therefore seem unwise to make our exegesis of the Epistle depend on our own hypothetical conclusions, the more so as, whatever they are, they will not commend themselves equally to other scholars. Fortunately, the main tenor of the letter is plain, and the main lines of exegesis are quite independent of a detailed knowledge of the setting, although this would lend great point and interest to our study. Detailed discussion of some of the questions will be found at the appropriate place in the Commentary. Here, we can attempt only a broad summary to set the detail in its wider perspective.

I. THE EPISTLE'S DESTINATION

Paul clearly directs the Epistle to 'the churches of Galatia' (i. 2). He calls them 'Galatians' in iii. 1. In 1 Corinthians xvi. 1 he refers to an alms collection from 'the churches of Galatia'.

But does he mean ethnic Galatia or administrative Galatia? For the two areas are not the same.

A glance at the map at the back of most Bibles will show an unwieldy 'Province of Galatia' stretching right across the middle of Asia Minor. All scholars are agreed that the letter must be addressed to some group resident in that area. But from the contents of the Epistle it seems clear that Paul did not write this letter to any and every Christian who happened to be living in this huge area. He was writing to a definite public, probably a small public well known to him, consisting of the churches of a definite area. Where was this area? Was it the north of the province where the Galatians themselves lived? Or was it the south of the administrative area where Pisidians, Phrygians, Lycaonians, Jews and Greeks lived in a somewhat disorderly mixture? He can hardly have written to both groups at once; their circumstances, and therefore their problems, would presumably have been too different for that. Nor does there seem to be any other 'third area'. We are left, therefore, with mutual exclusives. Those who hold the 'North Galatian Theory' believe that Paul was writing to the Celtic inhabitants of the northern plateau who alone could be called 'Galatians' in the strict sense of the word. Those who hold the 'South Galatian Theory' believe, on the contrary, that his words were directed to the Hellenized 'mixed multitude' of the south who could be called 'Galatians' only by a doubtful courtesy, and whose territories might be loosely grouped under the geographical term 'Galatia' (though the Romans, in point of fact, never used 'Galatia' alone as a title for this province).

Let us first summarize, therefore, the main arguments used to support the North Galatian Theory.

1. This was the universal view of the Early Church. Presumably such a view was based on local church traditions now long lost to us; we may not therefore reject this argument lightly.

2. Paul addresses his letter to 'Galatians'; and that is what these northerners were by race and language. Not only so, but they lived in the true 'Galatia'. Other parts of the Roman

province would more truly be designated as Pisidia, or Phrygia, or Lycaonia, as the case might be—as Luke designates them in Acts. Indeed, as we have said, the official Roman title for the province was 'the Province of Galatia and . . . '— listing all these other areas in turn. This was not just another example of Roman 'fussiness'; it corresponded to the various historical stages by which the 'core' of the province, the old Galatian kingdom of the north, was gradually enlarged by various subsequent additions for administrative convenience.

3. It is argued that the characteristics described in the Epistle are those traditionally associated with the Gauls of the day of Julius Caesar. They are fickle, boastful, quarrelsome, immoral, lovable, exasperating. Would not all these qualities, and many more portrayed in Galatians, fit best those who are Celts by race and temperament?

4. Paul describes in this letter some of the circumstances connected with his initial evangelization of Galatia. None of these seems to tally with the account of Acts xiv which is indisputably the account of the evangelization of the southern area. Therefore he must be referring to the evangelization of some other area, and that can mean only the northern plateau. Paul says, for instance, that he evangelized 'Galatia' because of some sickness that befell him. This is manifestly not true of his southern visit, so it can refer only to some unrecorded visit to the north.

5. The plain reading of Acts either demands (Moffatt) or at least allows (the majority of modern scholars) a 'missionary journey' through this northern area on one or two occasions. What unrecorded trips there may have been from a base like Ephesus we can only guess. But we do not need to fall back on this old argument of 'the silences of Acts' to make such work possible.

6. Paul assumes that the majority, if not all, of his readers at 'Galatia' would be Gentiles. But there was certainly a very large Jewish population in the southern towns as is shown by the existence of synagogues in so many of them, and we know that there was a fair proportion of Jews within the churches there. In the north, by contrast, we do not know of any large

Jewish settlements, and therefore a Gentile church is, a priori, more likely.

7. A problem like that envisaged in the Galatian churches would be more likely to arise in the north than in the south, if indeed the basic problem is that of the right Christian attitude to the Law and the Covenant, especially to its 'sign' of circumcision. In the south, with large Jewish communities and a considerable Jewish element in the churches, such a problem would have to be faced squarely from the start before a Jew so much as believed in Jesus. There was little likelihood of its appearing later as a new and unexpected temptation to which the whole church succumbed.

Other arguments are used, but they are mostly either 'subdivisions' of those outlined above, or else mere refutations of 'southern' arguments. When set out in this way, the 'North Galatian Theory' seems unassailable; and so it remained until recent years. But almost as good a case can now be made out for the 'South Galatian Theory' and therefore, in fairness, the main arguments of its protagonists should also be set out in order. This can be done 'in vacuo', without reference to North Galatian arguments, although some will inevitably seem to be directly opposite conclusions drawn from the same facts.

1. We know of no churches at this early date in the north, either in the New Testament or outside it. It is not until comparatively late in Christian history that they appear, and they are small, unimportant, and (apparently) without any tradition of apostolic founding. By contrast, we do know of strong churches in the southern area. Indeed, we have a detailed account in Acts of their foundation. If such existed in the north it is strange that Luke never mentions them. It is freely admitted, of course, that Paul may have passed through the western tip of Galatia proper (the northern area) on a few occasions; all that is asserted is that we have no direct evidence for evangelism.

2. It is hard to see what common name Paul could have used to cover Pisidians, Lycaonians, and so forth, other than the provincial name of 'Galatians'. Whether or no the people themselves would have considered the name appropriate is

another question. Indeed, Paul usually uses the name of the Roman province in which churches are situated when he wants to describe them collectively. 'The churches of Asia' (1 Cor. xvi. 19) is a good parallel. It is more natural to assume that he follows this custom here too, rather than restricting his meaning to a mere geographical or ethnic district.

3. It seems more likely that the Judaizers would have pursued Paul in the southern regions rather than across the remote plateau of the north. We know that he had already met with Jewish opposition in the south. If Jews were turning to Christ, this would be intensified. Antioch was near; even Jerusalem was not too far away. What more natural than that emissaries of the Judaizers should have campaigned in the south?

4. Many of the details of the Epistle seem to fit the circumstances of the southern evangelism detailed in Acts. Attention will be drawn to these at various points in the commentary; some of them are tenuous, but the mention of Barnabas, as one apparently known to the Galatians, has weight. Barnabas could not have been in the north, and there is no reason why Paul should have mentioned him to northern Christians.

5. When Paul gives us a list of the various delegates who are accompanying him to Jerusalem, with the long-awaited gift from the Gentile churches to their Jewish brethren (Acts xx. 4), there is certainly one, and possibly two, from this 'south Galatian' region. On the other hand there is not one delegate from the northern region; yet we know from 1 Corinthians xvi. 1–4 that Paul had canvassed the matter in 'Galatia', wherever it was. This may be only a straw in the wind, but it is certainly capable of use as cumulative evidence.

6. The general unlikelihood of Paul's hypothetical evangelization of the northern region is often used as an argument. It is claimed that it would be against his usual strategy of concentrating on heavily-populated areas and natural centres, where the population was already Hellenized, and where there were synagogues with consequent groups of Gentile proselytes. This, however, is rather a subjective argument, and can be easily turned in the other direction. When we begin arguing about the relative likelihood of invalids travelling to north or

south, we have left the realm of sober discussion altogether.

What, then, may we say in conclusion? Perhaps the most cautious answer would be, We do not know; but it seems likely that the letter was written to the Christians of the southern cities. No-one would deny the possibility, even likelihood, of Paul's passing through the western edge of the true 'Galatia' further north. (It is unnecessary, with Lightfoot, to make one's case even more difficult to prove by assuming that Paul conducted evangelistic campaigns throughout the length and breadth of the area.) If he passed through, he almost certainly evangelized; but it is hard to see how he could have the close contact envisaged by Galatians as its background. On the other hand, we must not fall into the opposite error of seeing in every verse of Galatians a hidden reference to some incident in the south, as recorded in Acts. Even if we do have the story of the evangelism of these southern cities, we can be sure that it is in epitomized form. Therefore, when we come to try to fix the date of the Epistle, we must remember this uncertainty and leave room for wide alternatives. Admittedly, this is not wholly satisfying; it is not a tidy solution. But New Testament scholars nowadays are usually chary of the 'tidy solution' that obscures the true nature of the problem.

II. DATE OF COMPOSITION

Broadly speaking, our answer to this question will depend upon our answer to the first. If we follow the 'North Galatian' scholars, we must put the Epistle after Paul's first possible visit to the northern region. That, on one interpretation of the text, would be Acts xvi. 6, describing Paul's travels through Asia Minor on his way to Europe on the second missionary journey. But not all would agree that 'Galatia proper' is meant here; and few would feel, with Moffatt, that the text clearly states that Paul evangelized the region, whether or no he passed through it. Also, many older scholars have felt that the wording of Galatians iv. 13 (see the commentary) implies two visits of Paul to this region before writing the letter. If this is so, or if Acts xvi. 6 be not accepted as evidence, then Acts xviii. 23

would be the first possible occasion. This would be at some date after the second and before the third missionary journey. Therefore, even if we take the Northern theory, there is a considerable range of date involved, although at least the Epistle could not be written before the second missionary journey. How much later it is after any of these dates is yet another question. Because of the wording of Galatians i. 6 (see the commentary), many think that the letter must have followed the visit almost immediately. But this is not necessarily so. It is quite possible that a period of several years elapsed, though it is unlikely to have been so long. If we put the Epistle as written at some time during Paul's Ephesian ministry, we should have a leeway of two years and more (Acts xix. 10).

A great deal will depend on our view as to the relation of Galatians to 1 and 2 Corinthians and to Romans. If, with Lightfoot, we see it as later than Corinthians and earlier than Romans, then we must put it as written from Corinth, when the third missionary journey was almost over. If, on the other hand, we consider it as earlier than Corinthians as well as Romans, then we must put it early in the Ephesian period. Few responsible scholars would be prepared to put Galatians as later than Romans (of which it seems almost a 'rough draft'), so that any later date is most unlikely.

If we follow the Southern theory concerning its destination, then we could place the Epistle very early indeed. The southern area was already evangelized at the close of the first missionary journey, in Acts xiv. Even if we press the need for two visits, we could, at a pinch, see them as being the outward and homeward visits on this occasion (Acts xiv. 21). If we are sticklers for two separate visits, we could find the second visit in Acts xvi. 1, at the very start of the second missionary journey. No later missionary activity in this southern region seems to be recorded, so we can hardly date the Epistle much later than either shortly before, or shortly after, the so-called Council of Jerusalem in AD 49. If we opt for the Acts xiv visit, then the Epistle could be before the Council. If we decide in favour of the Acts xvi instance, then the Epistle is clearly after the

Council, for Acts xvi. 4, in the same context, describes how Paul delivers to the local churches the 'decrees' of the Council. Which of these are we to adopt? It largely depends on the question of the relation of the chronology of Acts to that of Galatians. We must therefore consider briefly this subsidiary question.

Stripped to its bare bones, the problem is this. Acts clearly records three visits of Paul to Jerusalem: ix. 26 (shortly after his conversion), xi. 30 (the so-called 'famine relief' visit), and xv. 4 (the 'Council of Jerusalem' visit). For all we know, there might have been others; but these at least are certain. As against this, Galatians records only two: i. 18, a first visit, and ii. 1, a visit with Titus 'fourteen years after'. We shall probably not be wrong in equating the two first visits. But is the visit recorded in Galatians ii. 1 the 'second visit' of Acts (the 'famine relief' visit), or the 'third visit' (the 'Council of Jerusalem' visit)? Obviously, this would settle the date as being either before or after the Council (with a third possibility, that the letter was actually written during the Council, or the preliminary discussions that may have led to it): thus we should be able, at a blow, to decide between Acts xiv and Acts xvi.

Some of the problems involved in such a decision will be discussed in the commentary. Here, it is enough to say that to see, with some scholars, Acts xi as a mere 'doublet' of Acts xv, is no solution. First, it is unfair to the general reliability of Acts, wherever it can be tested. Secondly, it still does not explain the main problem. If the Galatians ii visit is indeed that of Acts xv, the Council of Jerusalem, then why is the account in Galatians so different from the account in Acts? Even if there is an attempt to deal with this question in the same cavalier manner, by saying that Luke's account in Acts is inaccurate, the problem still remains. If the letter was written after the Council, then why does not Paul settle the question once and for all by referring to the apostolic decrees? He certainly was prepared to circulate them among the cities of this region, as can be seen from Acts xvi. 4. Even if hypercriticism denies that Paul actually did this, the question still remains in a slightly altered form. How could such a problem as that of Galatia arise at all after the Jerusalem decision? Whether the Galatians knew of it or not, the Judaizers certainly would have done so.

Once again, a definite decision is difficult. Robert et Feuillet wisely warn us not to seek a detailed synchronization, but to be content with broad outlines. Luke and Paul are speaking from different angles, to prove different points. Their emphasis and even selection of significant incident are doubtless different, and we do not have enough detail to attempt exact correlation. But, as an interim suggestion, it seems most unlikely that Galatians was written actually after the issue of the Decree. We may therefore place the Epistle as after the 'famine relief' visit—perhaps some little time after the first missionary journey, when the strife that will ultimately lead to the Council of Jerusalem has already broken out in the north. It might have been written from Antioch; it might have been written *en route* for Jerusalem, though this is less likely; it might even have been written from Jerusalem itself (as suggested above) in the whirl of discussion that seems envisaged in Acts xv. 7 before the actual Council itself. We will still be left with some problems as to Paul's 'telescoping' of events. But at least they are not insurmountable, and the general picture will make sense.

III. OCCASION AND PURPOSE

Again, at first glance, the answer is easy. The Epistle was written as an answer to the Judaizers who were troubling the Gentile churches of Galatia with their insistent demands that, to be a good Christian, one had first to become a good Jew. Circumcision and some law-keeping at least were necessary to salvation. Salvation is thus not by faith in Christ alone; it is by faith in Christ and by obedience to the law. Paul fought this tooth and nail as being a denial of the gospel that he preached. Is not this explanation clear, simple and satisfying?

Clear and simple it is undoubtedly. The only trouble is that it is too clear and simple to be ultimately satisfying. As far as it goes, it is true; and fortunately it will suffice us for a 'rule of thumb' by which to interpret the Epistle. But it leaves many questions unsolved, questions that rise directly from the letter itself. We may never be able to answer them satisfactorily. But the attempt to answer them may at least lead to some truths that can further help in the interpretation of an Epistle which is packed with spiritual dynamite.

Some of these questions would run as follows. Who were these Judaizers? Were they members of the local congregation or men from outside—perhaps from Jerusalem itself, though not sent by James? What relationship, if any, do they bear to the 'Jewish' (non-Christian) adversaries who pursued Paul equally relentlessly? That there was no relationship it would be hard to believe, although the groups are obviously different. Are they Jews at all? Or are they Gentiles, perhaps even Gentile proselyte converts to Christianity? Such men might have all the perfervid enthusiasm of new converts without the discrimination to be expected of those more mature in spiritual things, or those already with a Jewish background. As mentioned above, a Jewish Christian would have had to weigh all these problems carefully long before when he decided to be baptized. Was there some one well-known ringleader whose identity, though known to Paul, is deliberately suppressed in this letter, possibly for the sake of 'good relations' with the Jerusalem church? If so, who was he? We should dearly love to know the answers to some or all of these questions. Such answers would illumine the darkness of the history of the Church in the apostolic age, as nothing else could do. For instance, were they 'radical' Judaizers, or 'moderate' Judaizers? Did they actually say that the law was necessary for salvation, or only that it was necessary for perfection? But there is an even more interesting question, popularized by Ropes. This is the theory that Paul's battle in the Galatian churches was 'three-cornered', not a simple defence of the gospel against the Judaizers. In other words, he assumes that there was not only a 'Judaizing' party (either Jewish, Jewish-Christian, or Gentile-proselyte, as outlined above); there was also a Gentile 'pneumatic' party, rather akin to the later Gnostic movements. This group was anti-Jewish, but also antinomian and immoral.

Worse still, they may have represented themselves as championing Paul's gospel, and claimed him as their teacher. If Marcion could misunderstand Paul so grossly at a later period, why should not these Galatians do so at an earlier time?

It is unlikely that the situation was as clear-cut as such a reconstruction would suppose. But at least it is a useful warning to us not to over-simplify the position in the Galatian churches. The roughly analogous situation at Corinth shows how complex the cross-currents of Early Church life often were, and the Corinthian correspondence must date approximately from the same period, as we have seen. For a summary of the various theories of this type, Guthrie and Wikenhauser may be consulted. The various points that rise directly from the text of Galatians will be discussed at the appropriate places in the commentary. Metzinger contains very full bibliographies on most other aspects of the Galatian question, but not this particular point.

ANALYSIS

I. THE ARGUMENT FROM HISTORY (i. 1–ii. 21).

    a. Greeting (i. 1–5).
    b. The letter's subject introduced (i. 6–9).
    c. Paul's conversion (i. 10–24).
        i. Paul's protest (i. 10–12).
        ii. Paul's life before his conversion (i. 13, 14).
        iii. Paul's conversion and subsequent events (i. 15–24).
    d. Later relations with Jerusalem church leaders (ii. 1-10).
    e. The clash with Peter (ii. 11–16).
    f. Death and the new life (ii. 17–21).

II. THE ARGUMENT FROM THEOLOGY (iii. 1–v. 1).

    a. Introduction (iii. 1–6).
    b. Abraham's faith (iii. 7–9).
    c. Who is under the curse? (iii. 10–14).
    d. Does law annul promise? (iii. 15–18).
    e. What is the purpose of the law? (iii. 19–29).
    f. The difference between son and infant (iv. 1–11).
    g. A personal appeal for better relations (iv. 12–20).
    h. An argument from rabbinics (iv. 21–v. 1).

III. THE MORAL ARGUMENT (v. 2–vi. 18).

    a. The goal of the gospel (v. 2–6).
    b. A personal aside (v. 7–12).
    c. The true use of freedom (v. 13–18).
    d. The 'natural results' of natural man (v. 19–21).
    e. The harvest of the Spirit (v. 22–26).
    f. How to deal with the offender (vi. 1–6).
    g. Sowing and reaping (vi. 7–10).
    h. The autographed conclusion (vi. 11–18).

COMMENTARY

I. THE ARGUMENT FROM HISTORY (i. 1–ii. 21)

a. Greeting (i. 1–5)

'Paul, an apostle, not an apostolate from men, nor through man, but through Jesus Christ and God the Father, who raised Him from among the dead, and all the Christians with me here, to the churches of Galatia: grace to you, and peace, from God our Father and the Lord Jesus Christ, who gave Himself for our sins, to take us out of this present wicked age, in accordance with the will of our Father-God, to whom be the glory for ages of ages. Amen.'

1. *Paul* is the sender of this letter: the one simple word is enough to introduce him to the recipients. Any letter of the time will begin with the name of the sender, closely followed by that of the recipient. Normally, the bulk of the letter will be written by an amanuensis: it will be only in the closing lines that the author will pick up the stylus himself, and add a sentence or two in autograph. Forgery may well have been a danger in the days of Paul himself: certainly, in the sub-apostolic days, 'pseudepigraphy' became a menace.

Even without such evidence, it is doubtful if the Galatians were in any doubt as to the writer of this letter: from beginning to end, the letter breathes Paul. Not only might it be described as the earlier 'rough draft' of Romans, it also contains so many other Pauline idiosyncrasies that, along with Philippians and the Corinthian correspondence, it has always been regarded as belonging to the indisputably Pauline 'core'. Even those who nowadays attempt to solve the problem of authenticity by the use of electronic computers usually start with this Epistle as base.

Paul (in its full form of *Paulus* or *Paullus*) is a common enough Roman surname (never a praenomen or distinguishing name), found frequently in classical literature, inscriptions, and papyri (see Arndt-Gingrich). Even in the New Testament, the Sergius Paulus of Acts xiii. 7 bears it. Originally an aristocratic Roman name, it was later borne by many newly-enfranchised citizens, whether because their ancestors had originally been slaves of some member of this house, or as a compliment to some provincial governor. Perhaps we may compare the way in which Eastern or African Christians, when wanting to take a Western name in addition to their own, will frequently adopt either that of a much-loved missionary, or of some prominent Western statesman. Beyond the fact that Paul was born a Roman citizen, we know nothing of the origins of citizenship in his family. He certainly had no drop of Roman blood in his veins; but none made the proud name of *Paullus* more illustrious.

It is just possible that this was not the name used by his enfranchised family, but chosen by him because of its assonance with his Jewish name, Saul. Many instances of this sort of assimilation occur in the New Testament: Simeon ('Symeon' of the rv) appears in Greek as 'Simon' ('snub-nosed', a good Greek word). We do not know whether Paul continued to be known as Saul in Jewish-Christian circles; perhaps he did. Certainly when Peter is mentioned in Jewish contexts he is more commonly called 'Symeon' or 'Cephas'. Nevertheless, it is only before the first missionary journey that Luke uses this name to describe him. After Acts xiii. 9, he is always 'Paul'. It is as though his acceptance of the Gentile mission to which his conversion led him demanded the renunciation of his Jewish past. And his Jewish name, with its reminder of Saul, the first king, the pride of Benjamin, stands for that heritage. When writing to what are presumed to be Gentile, not Jewish, converts in Galatia, the name has peculiar appropriateness. He is reminding them that for Christ's sake he has identified himself with them.

But he is also *an apostle*. In spite of all the theological battles over this word in recent years, it is probably best to leave it. A word like 'emissary extraordinary' may recapture some of the atmosphere, but is too clumsy for use. To us, the word means first and foremost the twelve men chosen by Christ to be near Him, and whom He might send on His tasks. But the Scriptures merely say that Christ called the twelve 'apostles'; that is, He used an existing word to make clear their status and functions. To the Jew the word was well defined; it meant a special messenger, with a special status, enjoying an authority and commission that came from a body higher than himself. Thus in the days of the New Testament the word had a meaning far wider than 'the Twelve' (or sometimes 'the Eleven' after the defection of Judas). It may be used of the Twelve, but it may also be used of James the brother of the Lord (not in any list of the Twelve), and of a wider, indefinite group.[1]

Yet Paul uses it here bluntly and deliberately, not merely to inform them that this letter is from 'Paul the missionary' as distinct from any other Paul. It is from Paul the apostle as distinct from the body at Jerusalem, the members of which equally call themselves apostles. Yet to him 'apostle' is not so much a title as a description, and he makes that plain by what follows.

His apostolate, he tells them, is 'not from men nor through man' (RSV). It has neither human source nor human agency (NEB, 'not by human appointment or human commission'). There is probably no significance in the change from *men* to *man*. Paul may be recalling, however, that a Jewish *apostolos* would normally be sent from a group (perhaps the Sanhedrin) and would have received his commission from the high priest or some similar high official. When Paul went on his journey to Damascus his apostolate was of this nature (Acts ix. 2). No longer is it so; it is *by Jesus Christ, and God the Father*. It is from this source that he has received his commission. It is impossible to say how far '*Christos*' had advanced in the direction of becoming a proper name, as it is in modern English; usually in the New Testament, when it has no definite article, it is so treated. With the article it is probably better translated 'the Messiah' or 'the Anointed'. But the important thing is that for Paul the source of his authority is Christ; and this is a Christ deliberately put side-by-side with God. Among ancient wit-

[1] For a detailed discussion see the Appendix in Burton.

nesses only Marcion the heretic omits *and God the Father*; and this was certainly from doctrinal considerations.

In Paul's writings it is rare to find an unqualified reference to God. He is usually further characterized at once as the God who revealed Himself in such-and-such a way. Normally, this is in connection with His work in and through Christ; and this passage is no exception. He is the God *who raised him from the dead* (this is the normal New Testament form of expression, rather than to say that Christ rose from the dead). Always in the New Testament the resurrection of Jesus Christ is seen as the supreme proof of the power of God. That is why belief in the resurrection of Christ is central to the Christian faith. And since Paul sees the Christian life in terms of sharing in the death and resurrection of Christ, the point has an even greater relevance for him.

Why does Paul describe himself in this way? Certainly not in opposition to the apostles at Jerusalem, for they did not owe their commission to man any more than he did. They too could have claimed that they were appointed by Christ in accordance with the will of God the Father. Rather his aim is to show that his apostolate stands or falls with theirs; it rests on exactly the same basis. It is extremely unlikely that any of the Jerusalem apostles 'stood on their dignity' *vis-à-vis* Paul. But it is highly likely that some of their more enthusiastic followers did so. We know, for instance, that they frequently accused Paul of being no true apostle, or, at best, a self-appointed one. No man who reads the story of his conversion could take this charge seriously; and perhaps this is why Paul so often refers to it in his own defence. Indeed, the whole of the first part of this Epistle will be an appeal to history, first and in particular to Paul's own personal history, and secondly to the history of his relations with the Galatian churches.

In modern terms, the validity of Paul's 'orders' is being questioned. He replies by showing that, put in this way, the question is an improper one to ask since, in asking it, the questioners condemn themselves also. If the Jerusalem apostolate and Paul's apostolate to the Gentiles (and, indeed, Peter's to the Jews) have all the one source, how can such a question even be asked? It was, it is true, the sort of question that greatly exercised first-century Jewry. Both John the Baptist and Christ Himself had been asked by what official authority they acted. Both had made the same answer, whether explicitly or implicitly; it was the authority of God. It found its proof and vindication in the working of God through them. And this is ever Paul's thought too. The proof of the 'validity' of his ministry is to be found in the working of the Holy Spirit that accompanies it, in the results of a ministry rather than in its antecedents. If any at Jerusalem should challenge this, they would at once be aligning themselves with Jewish theology rather than Christian. And is this not equally true today?

2. But Paul does not write alone. *All the brethren which are with me* (NEB, 'I and the group of friends now with me') also join in the salutation. Much study has been devoted to 'Paul's travelling circle' in recent years, of which Judge's little book[1] may be singled out. While it is true that there are a few Christians whose names appear constantly in connection with that of Paul on his travels, we should beware of seeing him as some sort of stoic philosopher, surrounded by an eager circle of pupils. The casual translation of NEB may well be correct, rather than the views of those who emphasize the distinction between this 'inner circle' and the main body of the church, usually called 'the saints'. But 'friends' is inadequate for *adelphoi*, 'brothers'. The word has a long history in Judaism, as may be seen from the Old Testament. In the new Christian family it took on a richer and deeper meaning. Brothers, saints, chosen, Nazarenes, Galilaeans, Christians: the names were legion, but the sense of 'belongingness' was common to all. True, Paul often does associate some younger member of his circle with himself in the writing of an Epistle. But it is unlikely that the association extends further than the greeting in this case, the more so as in verse 6 Paul will drop at once into the first person singular. Probably he wishes to show the

[1] E. A. Judge, *The Social Pattern of the Christian Groups in the First Century*, 1960.

Galatians that Paul does not stand alone in opposition to the Judaizing heresy that has crept into the churches of Galatia; he speaks for countless simple Christians everywhere.

The letter is addressed *unto the churches of Galatia*. It was an adequate address in its day, but has puzzled scholars sorely since. For a summary of different views see the Introduction.[1] Whatever the exact geographic location it clearly refers to a number of local *ekklēsiai* or 'churches', that form part of the one great *ekklēsia* or Church. This is consonant with Pauline usage throughout. If this is a circular the question arises as to whether only one copy was sent, or several. If only one copy was sent, presumably the local churches were expected to hand it on from one to another when read, possibly making transcripts themselves. In view of vi. 11, where stress is laid on the handwriting, it seems impossible that there was more than one autograph copy. Paul elsewhere exhorts local churches to pass on and share with one another such apostolic letters of general interest and relevance.

3. The greeting is *Grace be to you, and peace*. The juxtaposition of these two is thoroughly Jewish and was now to become thoroughly Christian. It is a mistake to see here a junction of the Hellenic and Semitic worlds. It seems as if Paul at first had only intended to say 'Grace be to you', and then added 'and peace', almost as an afterthought. As for Paul, *charis* ('grace') is almost synonymous with 'Jesus Christ' (for he knows nothing of impersonal grace), and as we enjoy peace with God through Him the distinction is not great. 'Peace' is the Greek *eirēnē*, the promised gift of Christ to His troubled disciples; it is the Hebrew *shālōm*, that sense of spiritual well-being that comes from right relationships with God. Wherever Arabic has brought the greeting 'salaam' across the world, there is at least a verbal echo of this great truth.

This grace and peace come 'from God our Father and the Lord Jesus Christ' (some MSS reading, as in AV, *from God the Father, and from our Lord Jesus Christ*). It is probable that by the common construction known as chiasmus (which could be

[1] Pp. 15 ff.

translated 'x-shape') the source of grace is seen as Christ, and the source of peace as God the Father. Again, however, the main theological point is the close association of Christ with God. Indeed, the use of the word *Kurios*, 'Lord', as a title of Christ would in itself be sufficient to assure this. Much study has been devoted to this Greek word, the one chosen by the translators of the Hebrew Bible to stand for the divine Name in the original. It varied in meaning from the polite 'Sir' of address to a stranger up to the full confession of the deity of Christ. When the early Christians used 'Jesus is Lord' as a baptismal confession, they cannot have meant less than this.[1]

4. As Paul has particularized God the Father as the One who raised Jesus Christ from the dead, so here he particularizes Christ as the One who *gave himself for our sins* (NEB, 'sacrificed himself'; but this seems to give *dontos* too narrow a meaning, correct though the interpretation may be). Is Paul thinking of the supreme self-giving of Christ on the cross *huper*, 'on behalf of', our sins? If so, then the thought must be that of the sin-offering. Or does he think of the continual self-giving throughout the life of Christ? In that case, the Suffering Servant of Isaiah liii will be in his mind. But there is no contradiction, and both may be included. This is not a theological definition, but a confession of infinite indebtedness.

This self-sacrifice of Christ (for Calvary, not Bethlehem, is the centre of Pauline thought and theology) is always seen as producing a positive result. Here, the purpose is stated as 'to take us (NEB, 'rescue us') out of this present wicked age'. The division between 'the present age' and 'the age to come' was familiar to every Jew. What we are accustomed to translate as 'everlasting life' was to him 'life of the age (to come)'. In John's Gospel, the thought that this present age is under the power of the evil one is frequent. Thus, what Christ's death has done is to transfer the Christian from the sphere of Satan's power to that of God. While still living in this world, therefore, he enjoys already that life of the age to come. This is the victory of the cross to Paul. But it is just possible that the

[1] See Arndt-Gingrich under this word.

35

Judaizing heresy that was troubling the Galatians made great play of the Greek word *aiōn*, 'age', as the later Gnostics certainly did. In that case, Paul would be deliberately using a word familiar to his opponents, and showing how even this is caught up into the wonder of the Christian gospel. There are two ways of defeating an opponent. One is to show that his ideas are incompatible with revealed Christianity; the other is to show how they are both embraced and transcended therein.

But lest he should, even unintentionally, give the impression that atonement was the unaided activity of God the Son, Paul hastens to add that all this was 'in accordance with the will of our Father-God' (for there is but one article for both *Theou* and *Patros*). Here is no possibility of unreal antithesis between a harsh Father and a loving Son. The action of the Son was the very proof of the Father's love, as John iii. 16 makes clear. Christ came to fulfil the Father's will, and thus to reveal Him. The concept of *to thelēma, the will of God*, is one of the deepest in the whole New Testament. This rescues our Christian calling from subjective response, and roots it deep in the mind of God.

5. To any Jew it was natural to slip into a reverential *berākhāh*, 'blessing', after any mention of the divine name. 'The Holy One—blessed be He' is one of the commonest in later Jewish commentators. So here, after the new name of God, it is natural to add 'to whom be the glory for ages of ages' (where the same word *aiōn* is used). Just as in old days the name Yahweh with its memories of salvation from Egyptian bondage stirred a Jew to praise, so now the name of Jesus Christ stirs Paul to similar response. If the Jew of old was a 'Yahwist', to use the modern theological jargon, then Paul and those to whom he wrote were Christians. Their whole understanding of God was dominated by the revelation in Christ.

It is just possible that this should be translated not so much as an ascription, but as a glad affirmation: 'His is the glory . . .' In that case, we might compare it with the customary ending of the Lord's Prayer which, whether part of the original or not, certainly represents a very early liturgical 'response' like that of Paul. In either case, *doxa* is not the empty praise that man can give: *doxa* is the Hebrew *kābōd*, the unutterable effulgence of the divine glory, the *shekīnāh* that to a Jew denoted the very presence of God.

The *Amen* at the end (like *Hosanna, Hallelujah, Maranatha* and *Abba*) is one of the 'fossilized survivals' of Hebrew and Aramaic language of worship, transmitted through the New Testament Greek-speaking church to the later Latin-speaking church, and ultimately to most languages of earth. See Arndt-Gingrich on this word, usually translated in the LXX as *genoito* (we may compare Paul's common *mē genoito*, for the negative wish) with the sense 'let it come to pass'. When the old-fashioned Cantonese-speaking Christian says at the end of a prayer *shing sam shoh uen* ('with all my heart this is what I wish') he approaches very nearly the original Hebrew meaning. It may be, however, that the Hebrew word contained overtones, referring not only to the steadfast faith of the one who prays, but also the changeless faithfulness of the One to whom the prayer is made.

b. The letter's subject introduced (i. 6–9)

'I am astounded that you are so quickly turning away from the One who called you by Christ's grace—to a different gospel. Not that there really are two sorts of gospels; it is only that there are certain parties who are throwing you into confusion, actually aiming at the distortion of the gospel of the Messiah. But even if it were I myself, or a very messenger direct from heaven, who should bring a gospel to you other than the one that I actually preached to you, you must turn in horror from him, as being one under God's curse. As we have already told you, so now I repeat: if anyone is preaching a gospel different from that which you received, let him be under God's curse.'

6. After the opening greeting, Paul normally moves onwards to some prayer for the local church. He very often finds first some point on which he can commend them. Then he gradually introduces the real purpose of the letter, which is not always so pleasant to the recipients. All this is not only the normal construction of a first-century letter, but the typical pattern of Eastern politeness. But on this occasion there is no easy and gradual transition: Paul is too deeply moved for that. *I marvel*, he begins: it is incomprehensible to Paul's open nature that men should be capable of such conduct as the Galatians; *thaumazō*, 'I am astounded', is a strong word, and Paul means it. What conduct is it that so moves him? Not gross moral lapse, but that 'you are so quickly turning away from the One who called you by Christ's grace to a different gospel'. For *metatithesthe*, 'turning away', other suggestions are 'changing your mind' or even 'deserting' (see Arndt-Gingrich). The verb is present tense. This is a process which is still taking place as Paul writes: he may not be too late to arrest it. Also, it is probably middle voice, not passive. This is something that the Galatians are doing themselves; they cannot say that they are compelled to it by others.

All this increases their culpability, and every other clause in this verse is another whiplash. They are doing this *so soon*: it is not that with lapse of time the gospel has lost its freshness. Some scholars on the basis of the *houtōs tacheōs* have attempted to fix the date of the Epistle more exactly. But Paul may not mean 'so soon after I have evangelized you' (though this seems the simplest interpretation). He may mean 'you have capitulated to these false teachers so soon after their arrival in Galatia'. There had been no long struggle in which the Galatians had been gradually worn down. They had not only surrendered at once but had become enthusiastic over this new gospel. Whether or no this corresponds to some racial characteristic of the Galatians, it is difficult to say. But in many areas of the Younger Churches where response to the gospel has been swift, so has the lapse into heresy. *Him that called you* is, of course, God, not Paul. The apostle was but the herald, the ambassador, who brought the proclamation of the gracious offer. The Galatians have not abandoned a theological position; they have abandoned a personal, loving God, who has manifested that love in *the grace of Christ*. Elsewhere, Paul can speak of Christians being chosen 'in Christ'. Since Christ is the very grace of God personified there is no contradiction between the shorter and longer forms. It is typical of Pauline theology that *kalesantos* 'called' is an aorist participle. God's call to man is decisive, and demands a response. Perhaps there is a grain of comfort here for the Galatians, if they are ready to receive it. We might translate, 'who called you once and for all'.

Some ancient witnesses to the text read only 'him who called you by grace' (so NEB); this makes no real difference. Others read 'from Christ who called you by grace'; but this, while equally true, is not a typically Pauline phrase.

Paul sees the teaching of these Judaizers as *another*, or 'a different', *gospel*. We may leave the consideration of their actual teaching until later in the Epistle where Paul seems to be dealing with it in some detail. Here we may simply ask, Is Paul not being narrow-minded? After all, these Judaizers certainly preached salvation through Christ. They never denied, as far as we know, that it was necessary to believe in Jesus as Messiah and Saviour. How, then, can Paul say that this is a 'different gospel'? It is true that the Judaizers seem to have had certain rites and ceremonies unknown to the Gentile churches founded by Paul. But did this really mean any more than the 'denominational differences' in Christendom today? One church may use written forms of prayer, while another prefers extempore prayer; but we do not normally think of denying to our brethren the name of Christian because of this. Furthermore, it is highly likely that the Judaizers observed no customs other than those observed by the bulk of the church at Jerusalem; and Paul certainly never accused James or John or Peter of preaching 'a different gospel'. Indeed, his whole point in this letter is that Jerusalem and Antioch preach exactly the same 'good news'. Why then is he so vehement in his opposition to the Judaizers?

7. Perhaps the best way to see why Paul attacks their teaching so vigorously is to read the next few clauses. He has said that this Jewish-Christian preaching is a 'different gospel' (*heteros*, properly in Greek 'another of two alternatives', although in Hellenistic Greek such finer distinctions are blurred[1]). He now goes on to say that it *is not another* (*allo*): it is only that there are some men who *trouble you*, who are 'throwing you into a state of mental confusion' (*tarassontes*) and actually want to pervert the gospel of the Messiah. There are several possible interpretations of this sentence. It is probable that for a moment Paul has given this false teaching the name *euangelion*, 'gospel', and that he now wants to retract this name. A different gospel? How can there be any such thing if there is only one gospel truly so called? There can be only a distorted gospel, not another gospel. But, in so saying, is Paul allowing that the Judaizers preach essentially the same gospel, distorted though it be? Or is he condemning them outright? The latter seems the more natural interpretation, but the two need not be mutually exclusive. No men were more sure that they preached 'the gospel of the Messiah' than these Jewish-Christians. But no men mangled the gospel more. There may be a deeper stress in the *thelontes*, 'want to' (RSV): Paul may mean that this is a wilful distortion of Christian truth, and thus the more culpable (although in the Bible all spiritual blindness is seen as wilful). Alternatively, he may mean that, while this is their desire, they cannot succeed. For all their distorted presentation, the gospel remains, eternally valid, eternally the same. *Tarassontes* (NEB, 'who unsettle your minds') is an interesting word. The various forms of this root always describe the opposite of that typical gift of Christ, *eirēnē*, peace of heart. A 'Galatian gospel' can bring only unsettlement, doubt, lack of inner harmony, because it strikes at the heart of the great New Testament doctrine of assurance of salvation.

Who are the trouble-makers? *Tines*, *some*, is vague in the Greek—perhaps deliberately vague—even in the use of the uncompromising plural. Elsewhere in the letter Paul uses the singular, as though it were one particular person who is to blame. We cannot tell who they were; we do not know whether even Paul himself knew. But it is fairly likely that the source of the trouble was the extreme 'right-wing' group of the Jewish-Christian Church, probably emanating from Jerusa-

[1] See Arndt-Gingrich.

lem, though no doubt James was perfectly right in disclaiming any official connection with them (Acts xv. 24).

8. Paul's answer to this challenge is direct. The Galatians must learn to pay no attention to the outward qualifications of the messenger. No doubt they had been over-awed by these august figures from the 'mother church', who seemed to claim apostolic authority for their message. So far from receiving them, they must not even receive Paul himself if he should return preaching a gospel like this. When we realize the closeness of the link that bound Paul, the lonely bachelor, to his converts and the esteem in which they held him, we can appreciate the force of this injunction. It is not just that Paul, in a burst of spirituality, is begging his 'children' to correct him if he is ever wrong. The principle goes far beyond this. He is teaching them that the outward person of the messenger does not validate his message; rather, the nature of the message validates the messenger. Later, he will stress this again. The test of 'apostolic ministry' to Paul is to be found in the fruits.

But Paul is not content to remain here. Even if *an angel from heaven* were to preach any gospel to them other than that which they had received, Paul's wish is that such a man should be *anathema*, which conveys the same idea as the Hebrew *ḥerem*, 'under the curse', 'under the wrath of God'. From a man or object under God's curse the Galatians should turn in horror: so ought they to turn from preachers such as these. But this is the very opposite to what they have done. They have in fact listened with 'itching ears' as in 2 Timothy iv. 3.

Why the 'angel from heaven'? It may be that Paul is thinking of the general meaning of *angelos*, which is 'messenger': from any such messenger, whether human or apparently divine, they must turn away. It may be, however, that it is a reference to the Judaistic nature of the heresy. It was common Jewish belief that the law had been given through angelic mediators, and these new teachers may have stressed this point when urging the simple Gentile Christians to keep the law. Later Judaism, especially when tinged by Gnosticism, made greater play still of angels. Again, Paul may be using this word to show them the possibility of Satan himself appearing as an angel of light to deceive them. It was on the hearing of a false gospel, a gospel without a cross, that the Lord said 'Get thee behind me, Satan' (Mk. viii. 33). If, on the other hand, this letter was written to those living in the southern part of the Roman province of Galatia, then *angelos* may be a reference to the circumstances of Paul's evangelism of them (see Acts xiv. 11). For *euangelion*, 'gospel', see Arndt-Gingrich: 'originally a reward for good news, then simply good news . . . also in religious use . . . in our literature only in the specific sense God's good news to men, the gospel.'

9. Perhaps Paul fears that the Galatians do not yet understand the seriousness of the matter, so he reiterates it. *As we said before, so say I now again, If any man preach any other gospel unto you than that ye have received, let him be accursed.* There is probably no significance in the switch from plural to singular in the sentence. In the New Testament, the plural 'we' is often used for the singular 'I'.[1] In modern English, the 'we' has an authoritarian sense; but in some Eastern languages, the use of 'we' is more modest than the use of the blunt 'I'. If we have adopted the 'South Galatian' theory as to the letter's destination, then we may say that Paul's mind is going back to the time when Galatia was evangelized by himself and Barnabas (Acts xiv), and he is pleading with them to remember their united gospel on that occasion. In that case, the 'already', conveyed by the preposition *pro-* before the verb, would refer to the circumstances of their initial evangelization, and we would have to assume that Paul warned them from the start about the possibilities of subsequent distortion of the gospel. We cannot say that this was impossible, in view of his similar warning to the Ephesian elders delivered at Miletus (see Acts xx). Nevertheless, it seems more likely that Paul is referring to his own statement in the sentence before. He is simply saying, 'Let me repeat what I have just said.' That Paul would cheer-

---

[1] See Arndt-Gingrich under the word *egō* for literature dealing with this question.

fully repeat advice or instruction we know from his own words in Philippians iii. 1.

The *ho parelabete*, 'which you received', is an interesting phrase. In one sense Paul's own experience represents a decisive break with religious tradition, seen in its Jewish form. He will describe himself, before conversion, as 'a great traditionalist' (i. 14). Further, in the Gospels Jewish religious leaders are accused of neglecting God's plain command in order to keep their own cherished 'denominational' traditions (Mt. xv. 1–6). This is a continual danger before us all— especially those of us who are conscious of belonging to groups such as the Jews, with a long history of use by God. But Paul does not condemn all 'tradition'; what he condemns is tradition in conflict with the word and command of God. When tradition is 'independent', when it is not under the continual judgment of the word of God, then alone it comes under utter condemnation. Elsewhere, Paul commends churches for observing the 'traditions' that they have received from him (2 Thes. ii. 15), whether by word or letter. But the word *paradoseis* in that context seems to refer to 'handing down of doctrine', not of practices or of orders in the Church. It is thus not untrue to say that the only 'apostolic tradition' known in the pages of the New Testament, and commended there, is in the realm of doctrine. Those who hold that, hold the true 'apostolic succession'.

In the passage immediately before us, the aorist tense of *parelabete*, 'you received', while it should not be overstressed, probably conveys something of the thought of the 'once-for-all' nature of the faith delivered to the saints. Paul preached; they received. That was a decisive experience.

There are two other points that we should note here: the first is that the Judaizers would have undoubtedly laid great stress on 'tradition', as Paul the Rabbi knew well. He must meet this emphasis by showing that, in some circumstances, 'tradition' can become a stumbling-block, as it had been in his case and still was with the vast majority of his fellow-countrymen. But Paul is never content with a mere negative attack. His second point will be that his gospel is the true biblical 'tradition', for it goes back to God's promise to Abraham, centuries before the giving of the law.

c. Paul's conversion (i. 10–24)

The gospel is a truth; but for Paul and the Galatians alike it is far more than an abstract truth. It is a truth in experience, and Paul's most powerful argument will be to recall to the Galatians their own rich spiritual experience in early days compared with their present spiritual poverty. After that, he will turn to theological argument, using the very Old Testament scriptures that the Judaizers were doubtless quoting to great effect. Finally, in the closing chapters, he will use his closing argument —the transforming moral power of the true gospel. These are arguments that none can gainsay; but before he uses any of them, he will appeal to the undoubted facts of his own experience.

i. Paul's protest (i. 10–12). 'Now when I talk like this am I trying to win men's approval—or God's? Or am I trying to please mortal men? If I were still trying to give satisfaction to human master, I would not be Christ's servant. I pronounce solemnly to you, fellow-Christians, that the gospel which was preached by me is no human gospel. The proof is that I neither received it by human tradition, nor was I taught it by rote: it came through an unveiling of Jesus Christ.'

10. There is probably considerable stress on *arti*, 'now'. It seems likely that the Judaizers accused Paul of being 'all things to all men', in a sense very different from that in which he used the phrase. They seem to have insinuated that when he was among Jews, he preached the need of circumcision and law-keeping in order to 'curry favour' with them (NEB). He was simply, they said, trying to 'canvass for their support' (NEB), doubtless conscious of his own insecure position as no true 'apostle'. In a like manner when he was speaking to Gentiles he preached freedom from the restrictions in order to increase his following among them. To them Paul was an ecclesiastical politician, not a theologian. He was simply canvassing for high office in the Church. Naturally, such an untrue charge must have cut Paul to the quick. He hated inconsistency above all else, as we can see from his summary dealing with Peter at Antioch recorded in ii. 11. But he has learned not to waste time over his own hurt feelings; he appeals to obvious facts.

Of course, no man in his senses could accuse Paul, in the writing of this letter, of going out of his way to curry favour with anybody. Indeed, if he had desired to antagonize the Judaizers and Galatians alike, he would hardly have used stronger language. So much is clear. But he is probably referring to something much wider than this letter. His whole life is open to their examination. Since his conversion he has deliberately renounced the aim of pleasing men in favour of that of pleasing God alone. He has long ago learned that to combine the two is impossible, and this was one of the first truths that he taught his converts (see Eph. vi. 6; Col. iii. 22). He was not alone in this. The Jerusalem apostles had enunciated the principle boldly in Acts v. 29, and several quiet sayings of the Lord lie at its root. So concerned is Paul with pleasing God that he not only refrains from seeking to please himself; he does not even judge himself (see 1 Cor. iv. 1–5).

There is a world of meaning in the short word *eti*, RSV, 'still'. Paul now sees clearly that the whole course of his life in Judaism was designed not only to win the praise of God, but also that of men. The religious man is often praised; the Christian very rarely. But Paul does not say these things to praise himself. He is simply saying, 'There was a time when this charge that they make would have been justified. But it was when I taught as they taught; it is not true now.' He brushes over the charge itself by simply showing the utter inconsistency of service of men (in the sense of trying to curry favour) with that unique and complete devotion to God which is the only fit response to the manifestation of God's love in Christ. A slave can have only one master; that was axiomatic in the Graeco-Roman world of the first century (cf. Mt. vi. 24).

11, 12. But surely Paul serves some human masters in the gospel? No doubt the Judaizers claimed that Paul learned the gospel from the apostles and elders in Jerusalem; he was dependent upon them for approval and support. How then could he challenge any teachers from Jerusalem, the mother church? It is the same sort of argument that has often been used in the past (and singularly without profit) by Unreformed Churches in controversy with Reformed. Admitted that Paul has had a personal transforming experience of Christ: but from where did that experience come? So Paul will outline the steps that led to his conversion and the experiences that immediately followed.

I certify translates *gnōrizō*, a word which often means 'reveal' (see Arndt-Gingrich). Hence NEB, 'I must make it clear to you'. What follows is a declaration of more than usual solemnity. Paul has a variety of words with which he introduces such 'statements at law'; this is one of them. Once again, it is noteworthy that the apostle does not try to defend some theological position; he simply appeals to the gospel which they, as well as he, know was preached at the first in Galatia with well-remembered results. But what does he mean by saying that it *is not after man, ouk estin kata anthrōpon* (NEB, 'no human invention')? Paul himself explains by saying that he did not receive it as a 'tradition', in the way in which Jewish beliefs and practices had been handed down. This is a direct blow to the Judaizers. But more follows. Neither was the gospel something learned by rote and repetition, as doubtless Paul had learned rabbinics in the school of Gamaliel at Jerusalem. This is a warning to us today not to over-stress the importance of *katēchēsis*, 'baptismal instruction', in the Early Church. No doubt it existed, but Paul is concerned here to show that no man can be educated into the kingdom of God. This was another blow to the claims of the Judaizers. Paul had not, he says, learned his gospel in the presumed catechetical schools of Jerusalem. Where then had he learned it? Through a *revelation* (*apokalupsis*, 'unveiling') *of Jesus Christ*, he says.

Is the *Iesou Christou* subjective or objective genitive? Is this a revelation made by Christ to Paul, or a revelation of the true meaning of the Christ, made by God to Paul? Perhaps it is better to leave the ambiguity in the English as it is in the Greek. Of the alternatives the second seems slightly better, but it need not rule out the first. On the road to Damascus Paul received a transforming revelation. The source of all revelation is God; and the content was Christ. From that moment, the veil that had obscured the Messiahship of Jesus was drawn away, and Paul saw clearly the true meaning of facts with which he had long been acquainted. It seems impossible that Paul could have lived in Jerusalem from boyhood (the probable meaning of *anatethrammenos*, 'reared', in Acts xxii. 3) without knowing at least the outline story of the life of Jesus. It is equally impossible that he should have persecuted the Church without finding out the interpretation which it gave to these facts. Indeed, some scholars have held, on the basis of 2 Corinthians v. 16, that Paul had met or seen Jesus in the days of His Jerusalem ministry. If, as is probable, Paul was a younger contemporary of Jesus, that is by no means impossible.

However that may be, Paul does not seem to be claiming any supernatural acquaintance with the historical facts of the gospel story. That seems equally true of 1 Corinthians xi. 23 ff., the passage that deals with the institution of the Lord's Supper. It is unlikely that any special revelation of such a nature was necessary in this area. But no man could see Jesus as the Christ without the illumination of the Holy Spirit. This was as true of Peter in Matthew xvi. 17 as it was of Paul; and Paul soon saw that this principle could be generalized. See 1 Corinthians xii. 3. This 'revelation' of the suffering Messiah, God's Son, and the 'Lord', is itself the gospel. And this no mere man can teach, however much he may desire to do it.

ii. Paul's life before his conversion (i. 13, 14). How then can Paul prove to the Galatians the essentially supernatural nature of the gospel he preached to them, and still preaches? He does it by direct appeal to his own known experience; no man can deny this.

'For you have heard about the sort of life that I lived when I was of the Jewish faith in days gone by—how I persecuted and raided the Church of God beyond all measure and proportion.[1] I was making great strides in Judaism, outdistancing many of my own age-group among my people, since I was a regular extremist where ancestral traditions were concerned.'

13. Paul is concerned to show that, before his Damascus experience, he certainly did not believe this gospel. Moreover, he was in no way disposed to believe it. So far from accepting it, he was infuriated by what he regarded as blasphemy. Later, he was to sum up this period of his life by describing himself as 'in pious zeal, a persecutor of the church' (Phil. iii. 6, NEB). How had the Galatians *heard*? There are several possibilities. First, since in Acts Paul refers on two occasions to his own conversion in some detail (Acts xxii and xxvi), he may well have done so when preaching to the Galatians. He is always ready to reinforce theology by experience, as in this Epistle. Secondly, the Galatians might have heard the news themselves, as a rumour spread from church to church. The conversion of such a notable opponent must have made a great impression (cf. i. 24). Thirdly, the Judaizers themselves may have mentioned it scornfully—'the man is only a convert', they may have said. 'Have you never heard that he actually used to persecute the Church in early days?' The fourth, and very Oriental, possibility is that this was the first that the Galatians had heard about the matter. Paul is then simply introducing his own experience with an apology for mentioning it.

Conversation translates *anastrophē*, a word very frequently used in the New Testament, always of 'conduct, way of life, moral behaviour', whether good or bad. Paul's use of the word *Ioudaismos*, 'Judaism', is full of pathos. It is not until the days of the apostolic fathers that it will be used in direct contrast to *Christianismos*. But it is quite clear that already Paul regards Judaism as a different religion. For him it belongs to the past, as already in John's Gospel 'the Jews' have almost become synonymous with 'the opposition' (see Jn. x. 31, etc.). The rejection of their promised Messiah had turned Judaism from the main course of God's plan and purpose to a stagnant backwater. It is unfortunate that the misplaced zeal of the

---

[1] See Arndt-Gingrich under *hyperbolē*.

mediaeval Church turned this plain statement of fact into a theological principle, and initiated that 'baiting of the Jew' that has been the shame of the Church of God in all centuries.

The word *ediōkon, I persecuted*, is the very word used in Acts ix. 4, 'Saul, Saul, why do you persecute me?' It has often been noted, especially in recent years, that the context comes very close to identifying the Church with the body of Christ, though no formal identification is made. But this has roots in dominical sayings like Matthew x. 40, 'He who receives you receives me', and does not necessarily represent any further doctrinal development. It does seem unlikely however that Paul could use this same word *diōkō* without being at the same time vividly reminded of his experience at Damascus. He could have brought out the point mentioned above (that persecution of the Church is persecution of Christ) by calling the Church 'the Church of Christ', as he usually does. But here he obtains the same effect by calling the Church *ekklēsia tou Theou*, 'God's company'. Opposition to the Church is not only opposition to Jesus the Messiah. A Jew, not accepting His claim, might perhaps make light of this. It is also opposition to God, the God who, in Old Testament days, had chosen Israel as His 'company', and who now has chosen the Christian Church, whether Jew or Gentile. This is again a direct challenge to the Judaizers. All the past, as well as the future, belongs to the Christian Church, not to them. This was a point that the early fathers delighted to make in controversy.

14. But Paul had other more solid qualities to commend him besides his zeal in persecuting the Church (of which it is unlikely that Gamaliel at least approved, see Acts v. 38). *Prokoptō*, translated above 'making great strides', is a neutral word in Greek. The apostle does not say whether this road was a good or bad way, but merely that he was far on his journey. If religion be seen as a race, a competition, then Paul was well ahead in the lead; NEB translates 'outstripping many of my Jewish contemporaries'. These latter are probably his fellow-students at Jerusalem. All the 'men of his year' could bear him witness, if only they were willing (cf. Acts xxvi. 5). But it was only a progress in Judaism, a national religion. And something of the accompanying inner torment of those days can be seen from Romans vii.

Such progress in a young Rabbi would be shown by increasing knowledge of, and practice of, the 'traditions' of Israel, the increasing body of material that had, over the centuries, grown up around the Torah like a protective fence. For us, this is summed up, first in the Mishnah, then in the secondary later collection called the Gemara, the two together forming the Talmud. Of it, in later days, the Rabbis would say: 'The Scriptures are water; the Mishnah, wine: but the Gemara, spiced wine.' How early this attitude had begun to develop, we cannot say; but passages like Mark vii. 6–13 suggest that it was not unknown even in New Testament days. It is probably these traditional explanations which Paul describes as 'ancestral traditions'. But some have preferred to translate as 'my own family traditions', and scent a reference to Paul's family connections with the Pharisaic party (see Acts xxiii. 6). Whichever explanation be adopted, Paul says that he was a *zēlōtēs*, a 'zealot'. He may be using the word in a general sense. But he may be thinking of the fanatical zeal displayed by the party in politics usually called 'the Zealots', who were finally responsible for the catastrophe that overwhelmed Jerusalem. Yet Christ had already numbered one such among His apostles; compare Mark iii. 18 with Luke vi. 15 (the *Kananaios* of Mark simply represents a Greek transliteration of the Aramaic name of the party, corresponding in meaning to the true Greek name *Zēlōtēs*). Now Christ is to number a second among His apostles whose fanatical zeal had been just as great, although in the realm of religion, not politics.

iii. Paul's conversion and subsequent events (i. 15–24).

'But when it was the gracious will of God, who had set me apart when I was an unborn babe, and called me through His grace, to reveal His Son in my case, so that I might preach the good news about Him among foreigners, at once I did not consult with any human being, nor did I make the journey up to Jerusalem to those who had been apostles longer than I.

Instead, I retired to Arabia, and then came back to Damascus. Then, after three years, I did go up to Jerusalem, to make the acquaintance of Cephas, and I stayed with him for about a fortnight. Not one other of the apostles did I see, except James, the Lord's brother. On my oath before God, what I am writing is true.

'After that, I went into the general area of Syria and Cilicia. But I was unknown by sight to the Christian churches of Judaea: all that they had heard was that their former persecutor was now preaching the good news which he had formerly tried to destroy, and they continually praised God for what He had done in my case.'

15. What changed this young man from a purblind follower of tradition to a servant of Jesus Christ? It was the gracious will of God. To Paul, the origin of all human salvation is in the mind and loving purpose of God. That is always his sheet-anchor. But he never denies the reality of the response to which man is called. Before Herod Agrippa he refers to this occasion, and immediately adds 'I did not disobey the heavenly vision' (Acts xxvi. 19, NEB). But all this is within the *eudokia* of God, His loving purpose of salvation to men. The clearest use of the noun is to be found in Luke ii. 14; and, while it is the verb that is used here, there is no theological difference.

Like Jeremiah, Paul is one set apart and called from his mother's womb, by the prevenient grace of God. This may refer to Paul's call to the prophetic office, in view of the parallel with the wording of Jeremiah (Je. i. 5). But it may equally refer to his whole Christian calling. Romans ix. 11 shows how strong a theological position Paul was prepared to adopt. Here, too, the reference is to unborn children.

16. In either case God's gracious purpose of salvation is accomplished by a revelation of His Son: that is His pattern, and it is true of Paul as of any other Christian. If we translate 'in my case', we preserve the ambiguity of the Greek *en emoi*. The NEB, somewhat periphrastically but perhaps wisely, translates both meanings side by side, 'to me and through me'. Again, there is no theological contradiction What begins by being a revelation of Christ to Paul becomes a revelation of Christ in Paul as the Spirit produces His fruits in unaccustomed soil. And as Paul preaches to the Gentiles the unsearchable riches of Christ, so Christ is revealed through him. In view of the fact that a consciousness of his task followed so closely on his conversion, probably 'through me' is the best translation, if we must restrict ourselves to one. For Paul is clear that the purpose of this revelation, this unveiling of Christ, was so that *I might preach him among the heathen. En tois ethnesin* is probably better translated, 'among the foreigners'; it literally means 'among the peoples'—with the meaning of non-Jewish peoples. If the Jew often added 'dog' to 'Gentile', we should remember, before condemning him, that until recently 'dirty' was a stock adjective in English to accompany 'foreigner'. Acts ix. 6 and ix. 15 show how early in Paul's Christian life was this sense of calling to the Gentile mission. The Galatians were not only his spiritual children: they were the fruits of his apostolate to the nations (again, compare Jeremiah i. 5), his 'letters of introduction' to those who asked him by what authority he preached. They were the Spirit's seal on his apostolate; they were in his peculiar sphere. No wonder that he reacted so violently against Jewish interference here.

17. There are some slight difficulties in fitting the events which Paul here says followed his conversion into the highly compressed account of Acts. But his point is that he retired immediately to think out by himself and for himself the implications of the new discovery. By *Arabia*, he presumably means the country in the vicinity of Damascus. This whole area was under the rule of Aretas at the time, and might thus be fairly so described. But the exact location is unimportant. It is important that, whatever part Ananias had played in his actual conversion, he did not even have his help or that of any other of the Damascus Christians at this stage. This is a further proof that the gospel is essentially supernatural. By the Spirit the first illumination came to Paul, and by the Spirit the light would grow. Paul would be already familiar, of course, with all the Old Testament scriptures dealing with the Messiah. He would probably also be familiar with the Christian use of such scriptures, from his old days of controversy. All that now remained was to rethink his whole position in the light of the new revelation. For this, not advice but quiet was needed.

If Paul felt no need of consultation with the Christians of Damascus, he felt still less need of consulting those of Jerusalem. To the argument of the Judaizers that the apostles were at Jerusalem, Paul could quietly make the retort that he was an apostle equally with them. He did not deny the priority in time of their apostolic calling; but, apart from the fact that they *were apostles before me*, he would admit no difference. If, as is probable, Paul in these words is referring to the 'inner ring' of the Twelve, and not to the wider and vaguer apostolic group, then an interesting point arises. Upon what did Paul base his claim to be an apostle in this peculiar, almost exclusive sense? Undoubtedly, upon the will of God and the call of Christ. In this he stood equal with them in every respect. But, in Jerusalem at least, they regarded it as an indispensable prerequisite for the apostolate that a man should be a witness of the resurrection of Christ.[1] And, without having met the risen Christ, how could this be? We can only say that Paul seems to have regarded his meeting with the risen Christ on the road outside Damascus as being just as 'real' as any confrontation of Christ by Peter or Thomas in post-resurrection days. He was thus just as truly able to bear witness to the reality of Christ's resurrection as they were.

The importance of this is considerable. For it means that, at least in a secondary sense, any true Christian today can bear similar testimony to the risen Christ. It is necessary to say 'in a secondary sense', not because their experience is any less real, but because Scripture is clear that the original apostles had a peculiar function in bearing this witness to the life, teaching, death, and resurrection of Jesus Christ (cf. Acts x. 41). Indeed, the very New Testament is the abiding record of the eye-witness testimony of this vital first generation. There was, in the eyes of the Jerusalem church, a further qualification

[1] For the qualifications, see Acts i. 22, where the question arises over the appointment of Matthias.

to which Paul could lay no claim. It was to have been in the company of Christ from the days of John's baptizing until the resurrection (Acts i. 22). Those who interpret 2 Corinthians v. 16 as an indication that Paul had met or seen Jesus during the days of His Jerusalem ministry,[1] might conclude that Paul would probably have answered in the words of that verse. Mere knowledge of the events of the life of Christ had for him paled into insignificance compared with the flash of spiritual insight by which alone man could rightly interpret those events.

18. Nevertheless, Paul would be the last person in the world to deny the importance of such knowledge: it was perhaps to gain it that he finally sought the company of Peter, one great 'fount of tradition'.

It is often Paul's way, after a vigorous denial of the kind he has just made, to introduce some qualification which is demanded by his rigorous sense of honesty, even if it might seem to be damaging to his case. So in 1 Corinthians i. 14, when he has roundly denied that he has baptized any at Corinth but Crispus and Gaius, by i. 16 he has added the Stephanas family, and possibly others. Here then he freely admits 'that after three years he did go up to Jerusalem to make the acquaintance of Cephas, staying with him for about a fortnight'.

Once again, we are faced with unsolved and insoluble questions of chronology. The *three years*, for instance, may be counted either from the date of Paul's conversion, or from his return from Arabia to Damascus. On first reading, the account in Acts sounds as if all these events took place in a few weeks. But we can tell from the speed at which events move in Acts that this is a highly compressed account. If we had the full history of Paul's movements in early years, we might well find that they present a far more complex pattern than that found in either Galatians or Acts. We do not know, for instance, whether this was the visit of Acts ix. 27 paid by Paul to

---

[1] For a different interpretation see R. V. G. Tasker, *2 Corinthians* (*Tyndale New Testament Commentaries*), p. 87. Cf. also NEB.

Jerusalem following his conversion (for verse 23 of this chapter warns us that 'many days' had passed, which might well cover three years), or whether it was the so-called 'famine relief' visit of Acts xi. 30.

If we take the biblical text at its face value, it must be the first visit, the more so as the second visit was apparently paid from Antioch, not Damascus. But again Acts does not actually say that Paul spent all this very early period at Damascus. It states only that the period ended and began with Damascus. Nor does it even say that, when expelled from Damascus because of the hostility of Jews and Aretas (possibly arising from Paul's evangelism not only in the city itself but also in nearby 'Arabia'), Paul went immediately to Jerusalem. Jerusalem is merely the next point at which the story is taken up. Nevertheless, on Paul's testimony, the main point is clear. For the first few formative years he had not even re-visited Jerusalem; and, by that time, Paul's gospel was fully developed. Indeed, we have seen that it was because of preaching this gospel that he had been forced to flee Damascus and seek refuge in Jerusalem. So he could hardly be said to owe his gospel to the Jerusalem church.

Nevertheless, fair is fair; Paul admits that he 'did go up'. No doubt the Judaizers would seize on this: let them seize upon it. He has an admission to make which will be still more damaging to his case. He did it 'to get to know Cephas' (NEB). The verb *historēsai*, while originally meaning something like 'to enquire of', means in Hellenistic Greek 'to visit for the purpose of coming to know someone' (Arndt-Gingrich). Paul meets the Judaizing attack by explaining why he visited Peter, and indeed, why he stayed with him 'a fortnight or so' (the *hēmeras dekapente* is a vague term of time). Still it was clearly not as 'prince of apostles' that he sought him; why did he want 'to get to know' Peter? It is tempting to see the reason in the sole qualification for apostleship which Paul was lacking. He had no first-hand knowledge of the life and ministry of Jesus save that which any outsider might have (even a dilettante like Herod Agrippa; see Acts xxvi. 26). Peter must have been a priceless fount of knowledge. Tradition makes him the source behind Mark's Gospel. Any man who spent a fort-night lodging with Peter must have heard much about the earthly Christ. The first Epistle of Peter gives some idea of the kind of reminiscence to which Paul would have been able to listen.

19. Be that as it may, having admitted that he met Peter, Paul will go no farther. He makes the astonishing point that *other of the apostles saw I none*, even though he was in Jerusalem and living in Peter's lodging there. It is not certain whether we should translate the next phrase as 'except James, the Lord's brother', or as 'only James, the Lord's brother'; it all depends whether Paul reckoned this James as an 'apostle' or not. One of the Twelve he was certainly not. He had not followed Jesus from John's baptism and was apparently brought to belief only after the resurrection, possibly by one of the appearances of the risen Lord. He therefore lacked one of the qualifications just as much as Paul did, and would thus have been useless for Paul's presumed purpose. In any case, apart from these two (whose presence seems demanded by Acts ix. 27) he met none of the apostolic circle. This, if true, would make the claim of the Judaizers slender.

20. Not only is Paul's statement conceivable, it also fits perfectly with the little that we know of conditions in the Jerusalem church of the day. For one thing, Acts ix. 26 men-tions specifically that all the disciples at Jerusalem (and this, no doubt, included the apostles) were terrified of Paul when he arrived. Those who remembered his persecuting activities of only a few years before might be pardoned if they suspected another trick. Christians in many parts of the world today are learning to be wary of 'false brethren' who turn out to be secret police informers. To our cost we can understand the disciples' reaction more easily than our fathers could. But for the introduction of Barnabas (presumably to Peter and James), it is very unlikely that Paul would have met even these two. We see then that it may not have been by Paul's own choice that his contacts in Jerusalem were so restricted, though no doubt at this later stage he realizes that God's hand was in it all. Perhaps the other apostles were not yet convinced. Alternatively, they may not have been in Jerusalem. We know extraordinarily little of the movements of these other, more shadowy, members of the Twelve apart from various late traditions. True, Acts viii. 1 tells us that the apostles did not join in the general flight after Stephen's death: but Acts xii. 1–3 suggests that only James, the brother of John, and Peter were in Jerusalem at the time of Herod's persecution. Certainly, the aftermath of that pogrom was that even Peter fled to 'another place', almost certainly outside Herod's jurisdiction (Acts xii. 17).

Whatever we may guess to have been the probable reason, Paul has given us the blunt facts. He must realize how unlikely they sound, for he adds (paraphrasing for the sake of clarity) 'On my oath, what I am writing is true'. After such a solemn assertion, we do well to pay special heed. Paul is not giving a casual account of his movements. Everything here depends on whether he has had prolonged personal contact with the leaders of the Jerusalem church before his own gospel was 'formed'. He denies this by what was a virtual form of oath to a Jew—more binding still to a Christian who followed his Lord's injunction (see Mt. v. 34).

21. So far, so good. Paul has proved his point that, in early days at least, he had no sustained contact with the acknowledged leaders of the church at Jerusalem. But had he perhaps had contact with them elsewhere? Or at least, had he had such contacts with the scattered local churches of Judaea? This question would become the more important if, as suggested, the Twelve were at this time scattered more widely. *Afterwards*, says Paul, *I came into the regions of Syria and Cilicia.*

If, as seems demanded, the visit to Jerusalem he has just described was the one recorded in Acts ix. 26–30, then Paul has omitted the brief stay at Caesarea, and is now referring to his return to Tarsus. He is at Tarsus in Acts xi. 25 when Barnabas seeks him out and brings him to Antioch to share in the ministry there. But it does not follow that he has remained in the city all the time. As it is certain that he had preached at Damascus (and probable that he had preached in 'Arabia') in the period immediately following his conversion, so it is very likely that he preached both in Tarsus itself and the surrounding area during this later period. Otherwise, it is hard to see at what point in Paul's recorded journeys he could have evangelized Cilicia; and this seems demanded by Romans xv. 18–23, *inter alia*. It is uncertain whether *ta klimata, the regions*, is to be understood in a broad sense as 'the general area', or whether it means 'the province of Syria and Cilicia' in which Tarsus was situated. This will have bearing on the meaning of the word 'Galatians', but is not directly relevant here. For even if it meant the Roman province, it is not necessary to assume that Paul preached in every corner of it. Antioch itself, for instance, was in Syria properly so called. And at various times, the province extended far enough to the south to include Jewish-Christian churches. All that is necessary is that Paul should actually have preached in this period, while he was still uninfluenced by any Jerusalem interpretations of the gospel, whether 'right-wing' (with the Judaizers), or 'central' (with James), or 'left-wing', with Peter, who may have observed the food laws in early days (Acts x. 14) but later bluntly called the law of Moses an unbearable burden (Acts xv. 10).

22. For *unknown by face, agnooumenos tō prosōpō*, NEB mg. has 'unknown personally', which is probably a better translation. Many members of the Jerusalem church had good reason to know what Paul looked like, after the persecution of Acts viii. But, since this persecution appears to have been confined to Jerusalem itself, it may well have been that the country churches of Judaea were indeed ignorant of Paul's personal appearance. If the traditional (but late) description be accepted, he was short, bald-headed, with bushy eyebrows and piercing eyes, while his legs were slightly bandy. Such a man would be remembered well.

The 'Christian churches of Judaea' is literally 'the congregations of Judaea which are in Christ'. The plural *ekklēsiai* is used to denote local expressions of the one great *ekklēsia*, which is its usual force. Our use of 'churches' to express 'denomina-tions' finds no warrant in Scripture. Nor is it true to say that what we call 'denominations' did not as yet exist, for certainly great differences of usage (and perhaps church government) existed between the Jewish-Christian churches (as of Jerusalem) and the newer Gentile churches (as for example of Corinth). In i. 13 Paul has spoken of the 'congregation of God'; here he uses his more common expression 'the congregation(s) of Christ'. It was perhaps necessary for him to add some such word to make clear their distinction from the purely Jewish synagogues. No reader of the Old Testament denied that these latter had an equal right to the more general title 'congrega-tions of the Lord'. The use of the word *Judea* here has bearing on the meaning of the phrase 'the Christian congregations of Galatia' in i. 2. If the one means a Roman administrative district, then the other ought to do so likewise.

23, 24. There is, however, another point which is sometimes forgotten. Not only was Paul unknown by sight to the Judaean churches, but also his gospel had not emanated from them. Yet they recognized his gospel at once as that which they preached, and as that which he had previously attacked when he persecuted them. This means that what Peter and James are recorded as doing in ii. 6, 7, the country churches of Judaea had done long ago. They had accorded Paul full status and recognition. This is inescapable logic if we take Paul's position that the message validates the messenger. And that this was the view of the Judaean churches is shown by their praise to God for what He had done in Paul. *They glorified God in me.*

d. Later relations with Jerusalem church leaders (ii. 1—10)

'Then, fourteen years later, I went up again to Jerusalem with Barnabas, taking Titus along with me too. (I went up because of a revelation.) And I laid before them for consideration[1] the gospel which I am preaching among the nations (though I did

[1] So Arndt-Gingrich.

this in private before the powers that be, for fear that by any chance my race might have been in vain, or still be in vain).

'But not even Titus, who was with me, for all that he was a non-Jew, was forced to be circumcised. But, because of the "planted" false Christians, who had wormed their way in, to spy on the freedom which we actually enjoy in Christ, with the purpose of bringing us into slavery—not for one moment did we yield ground to them, and become subservient: for our purpose was that the gospel truth might remain for you.

'But from those who seemed to be somebodies—it makes no difference to me what kind of people they were: God cares nothing about "face"—well, these seeming authorities had nothing to add. So far from that, because they could see that I had been entrusted with the Gentile mission as Peter had been with the Jewish mission (for the One who had worked through Peter to reach the Jews had also worked through me to reach the Gentiles), and because they recognized the particular spiritual gift that had been given to me, James and Cephas and John, the recognized "pillars", shook hands with Barnabas and me, as a sign that we were one, agreeing that we were to go to the non-Jews, and they to the Jews. Only they were anxious that we should continually bear "the Poor" in mind— and this was the very thing that I had been eager to do.'

1. Once again, an exact chronology is impossible if we are restricted to the evidence that we have. It is possible, though not certain, that Paul means *fourteen years after* his first visit; but it could mean fourteen years after his conversion. Either way, this represents a very considerable lapse of time. Paul has already engaged in the Gentile mission for some years and there is no question about the gospel that he preaches being fully developed. But does the *palin*, *again*, necessarily mean a second visit? Or could it refer to a third, or any subsequent visit? Undoubtedly this is so linguistically. But the whole point of the argument would seem to be lost if Paul has suppressed the account of a second visit and gone directly to a third visit. If the visit of i. 18 is that of Acts ix. 26, then this must be either the visit of Acts xi. 30 (the so-called 'famine relief' visit) or that of Acts xv. 2 (the so-called 'Council of Jerusalem' visit). If the chronological order of Acts be accepted, then the famine visit was before Paul's first missionary journey, while the Council visit followed it. But in either case, Paul had been engaged in Gentile ministry for some time (notably at Antioch, see Acts xi. 26), so that he certainly had a 'Gentile gospel' which might be discussed.

The mention of *Barnabas* is not decisive, as, according to Acts, he accompanied Paul on both visits. Some have seen the mention of his name here and elsewhere in the Epistle as a proof that the recipients lived in the southern part of the Roman province often, as we have already noted, loosely called Galatia (though not by the Romans). This is because Barnabas undoubtedly accompanied Paul during the evangelization of this area (see Acts xiii, xiv), while the hypothetical evangelization of the northern plateau must have taken place, if historical, long after the breach between Barnabas and Paul.

More radical biblical critics find the answer in saying that Acts xi. 30 and xv. 2 represent variant accounts of the same incident—that we have here a 'double', in fact. But this is an impossible view for those who have a high opinion of the historicity of Acts, a historicity borne out in recent years in many minor aspects.[1] That being so, we cannot say that Galatians refers to this one visit. But in that case what has happened to the account of the second visit? No man could suspect Paul of deliberately falsifying, the more so as he is virtually 'on oath' by his own choice. On a matter like this it is inconceivable that his memory could be at fault. He was not travelling so constantly to and from Jerusalem that he could accidentally miss out the account of one visit. And it is unthinkable that he should suppress the account of one visit in such a context. The only possibility, if this verse does refer to the Council visit and not the famine visit, is that Paul regarded the latter as completely irrelevant, since it had nothing to do with theological matters, and thus deliberately omitted it without any intention of deceiving.

[1] For details see Bruce, *The Book of Acts*, 1962.

2. But why did he go to Jerusalem at all? The Judaizers would be quick to pounce on this. Better late than never if he was at last recognizing the authority of Jerusalem. Perhaps he was even obeying a summons to explain his strange behaviour in the north? Paul's answer is quick and to the point. He *went up by revelation*. He does not say how this revelation came. It may have come directly to Paul, or through the 'group guidance' of the local church (as in Acts xiii. 2) or through some travelling prophet of New Testament days (as in Acts xi. 28). The New Testament never says that 'direct' guidance is more spiritual than 'indirect'; and Paul makes no such claim for it here. It is however true that the circumstances of the famine visit (Acts xi. 27–30) would seem to fit this wording better than the strife that preceded the Council of Jerusalem in Acts xv. 1–2. The 'revelation' would then be the prophecy, made by Agabus, of the coming famine in Judaea. But it would be unwise to be over-dogmatic. We do not know what were the exact circumstances of the appointment of the Antioch delegation in Acts xv, and it may well be that the voice of some local prophet brought guidance here too. Whatever the occasion of the delegation, Paul thus sees its true reason as the mind and will of God. But, having arrived there, he says, *anethemēn, I communicated* (i.e. 'declared', 'referred', 'laid before them for consideration') *that gospel which I preach among the Gentiles*. By this time they could not influence Paul's gospel: it was too late for that. They could either accept it or reject it; there was no other alternative. And they were to accept and acknowledge it whole-heartedly. He does not say whether this conference was the main purpose of his going up. If that was so, then the visit must have corresponded to the Council of Jerusalem with its attendant opportunities of talk with great ones. On the other hand, he may simply have seized the opportunity afforded by the famine visit to satisfy his own mind on this matter, the language perhaps inclining rather to this interpretation.

The use of *anethemēn* here is perhaps a deliberate echo of *prosanethemēn* in i. 16. Paul now goes out of his way to do the very thing that he had sedulously avoided long before. That is typical of Paul. The circumstances have now entirely altered, and he is not afraid to act in a diametrically opposite way. This is precisely what lays him open to the charge of inconsistency in the eyes of lesser men, and perhaps this is why he needed the assurance of a revelation before thus going to Jerusalem.

Even granted that he did thus go, and did thus discuss, he makes plain that this was not before the general body of the church, *but privately to them which were of reputation.* This was not some 'general synod' before which he was being brought to book; these were man-to-man talks between the acknowledged leader of the Gentile churches and two who were generally considered to be leaders of Jewish Christendom. *kat' idian, privately,* and *tois dokousin* are both significant phrases here. He will discuss later what he means by the latter, but the meaning 'influential men' is common. To those who see in this visit a reference to the Council of Jerusalem these words present a real difficulty. Everything was public there, in a highly controversial atmosphere. It is always possible to say that these private meetings either preceded or accompanied the main public discussion of the matter. So long as we do not think in terms of modern 'sub-committees', this is conceivable.

It is typical of Paul that he does not say that the danger was lest Jerusalem should fail to recognize his gospel as the same as their own, resulting in a rift in the Church. It is characteristic that he is careless of the approbation of man; the approval of God is all that he covets. He frequently uses *trechō, run,* in this moral sense (as indeed the Stoics had before him in their moral philosophy; see Arndt-Gingrich). 1 Corinthians ix. 24–26 is one instance; Philippians ii. 16 comes even closer with 'run to no purpose', while in Galatians v. 7 he will apply the metaphor to the Galatians themselves. It is also typical that he uses the occasion to point out gently that his gospel has not changed. As he runs now, so he ran then. It is the Galatians who have moved ground, not Paul. This will be important if, as is probable, the Judaizers are accusing him of being a shifty fellow, always adapting his gospel to his hearers.

3. The next three verses constitute a notoriously difficult passage, not made any easier by Paul's obvious emotional excitement which, as often, leads him into involved grammar and unfinished sentences. These, in turn, lead to some textual confusion; and thus the circle widens. It is clear that some group, presumably the Judaizers, had pressed for the circumcision of Titus the Gentile. It is also clear that Paul disapproved of this. We cannot be altogether certain, however, whether Titus was actually circumcised or no. With the whole gamut of Pauline thought before us, we can understand why Paul was willing to circumcise Timothy 'because of the Jews' (Acts xvi. 3) but was violently opposed to any proposed circumcision of Titus. Certainly it would not have been equally plain to the Judaizers. Perhaps it was not plain to Barnabas. But the important point was that it should be made plain to James and the great 'central block' of the Jerusalem church, who were 'orthodox Jewish Christians', but not Judaizers. The only serious textual difference here is that some early witnesses omit the *hois oude* at the beginning of verse 5. This has the effect of making it possible that Titus was actually circumcised. NEB mg. thus translates 'I yielded to their demand for the moment'. Verse 3 would then be translated 'Titus was circumcised—but not because he had to be circumcised—it was only because of . . .', etc. Paul would then be saying that, in what he later regarded as a mistaken moment of compromise, he had agreed to the circumcision of Titus as a gesture. As he looks back now, his anger boils over at the treachery of those who led him to take such a step.

Had Paul actually gone as far as this, his emotional excitement would be very understandable. Also, as far as Titus was concerned, the retreat could not exactly be described as 'temporary'. He was now for life a circumcised man and the Judaizers could point to him in triumph as a living argument for Paul's two-facedness. But there is another possibility. If Paul had originally agreed to the circumcision of Titus, and later refused permission, all conditions necessary would be met. Both Paul and the Judaizers might well be indignant with each other for what they would regard as 'bad faith', and the Jews could accuse Paul of inconsistency again. This explanation is possible whether or no we keep the negative in verse 5. For whether we translate 'I yielded for the moment' or 'I did not yield for a moment', the ultimate result was the same.

4. NEB paraphrases *because of false brethren* (probably correctly) as, 'That course was urged only as a concession to . . .' (although the marginal suggestion 'The question was later raised because of' is also possible). Who were these *pseudadelphoi*, 'false brothers'? As Paul has already addressed even the erring Galatians as *adelphoi*, 'brothers', in i. 11 (indeed, it is the only term of affection that he uses until much later in this Epistle), it is tempting to see in this a denial that these Judaizers are acting the part of 'brothers' at all. They are utterly lacking in love. So Arndt-Gingrich interprets the word, comparing its similar use of those who are undoubtedly Judaizers in 2 Corinthians xi. 26. But NEB may be right with its blunt 'sham-Christians'. In this case, Paul would be denying the very reality of their Christian faith. This is a serious charge; but Paul knew them far better than we can ever do. But why are these 'bogus Christians' described as *pareisaktoi*? The word means 'secretly brought in, smuggled in', and, if we press its passive force, it suggests that these Judaizers were 'planted' on the church by some person or persons outside. We would dearly like to know whether any great figure stood behind the Judaizers. It was certainly not James, the Lord's brother; it was equally certainly not Peter, in spite of one school of critical scholarship, now outmoded. It was possibly not any one great apostolic figure, but simply the large group of Jerusalem Christians who had belonged to the Pharisaic party (Acts xv. 5) or perhaps the large bloc of ex-priests (vi. 7), those 'zealous for the law' (xxi. 20). In any case, the *pareisēlthon*, 'slipped in, sneaked in', while equally uncomplimentary, is active in sense, not passive. The agents of the Judaizers were not unwilling participators.

It is not clear into what meeting or group these *agents provocateurs* had wormed their way. Presumably the reference is to the Jerusalem church, and not to that from which Paul had come to Jerusalem (which was Antioch on each of the two possible occasions). The book of Acts does not mention Titus at all, so that we can look for no help from there. But such a man might well have been associated with Paul in the largely Gentile ministry of Antioch. He appears constantly in 2 Corinthians as Paul's trusty agent (again, in a Gentile setting), and in the Epistle to Titus he is responsible for an almost purely Gentile church, that of Crete. Indeed, Titus must have been associated with Paul at Antioch (as he was at Corinth) or Paul could not have taken him up with him to Jerusalem. But that does not prove that the tussle took place at Antioch. The plain reading of this passage suggests that the strife broke out as soon as the party had arrived at Jerusalem—although it is hard to see how Judaizers could be spoken of as 'planted' on the Jerusalem church if that was their source. But if Paul regarded them as 'sham-Christians', he might have concluded that they had wormed themselves into that church—rather in the way in which the apostles suspected Paul himself of worming his way into the Jerusalem church in order to learn their secrets (Acts ix. 26). If only we could apply the reference to Antioch it would fit much better. For we do know that some Jerusalem brethren entered that church and caused strife immediately by their Judaizing doctrine. Indeed, it was such behaviour that had called for the Council (Acts xv. 1). Probably the answer is that Paul is really thinking of these men at Antioch, even if nominally describing his Jerusalem opponents.

Wherever they were (and ultimately they were the same group in any case), Paul is vehement that their whole purpose was only to peep and pry into Gentile Christian liberty and bring men back again into slavery, this time to the Jewish law. He will deal with this question at greater length in the next main section of the letter (the 'Argument from Theology'), so that the details need not detain us now. Of course, no Judaizer would ever admit that his purpose was to 'enslave'. He was no doubt genuinely shocked by the carefree attitude of Gentile Christians to the law of Moses, his own most treasured possession. It is highly likely that he thought himself to be enriching their spiritual lives immeasurably. But from his own experience Paul knew that it was but a return to slavery. True, the Galatians had not been slaves to this particular moral system before. As pagans they had had their own system of religion and morals. But a change of masters is not an escape from slavery.

5. Paul is not fighting this battle on behalf of himself; it is for the sake of his Gentile converts with the aim of ensuring that the gospel truth shall remain for their enjoyment. Judaizing is not another aspect of truth; it is a lie.

The passage ii. 6–10 is once again very involved, both in thought and language, although the difficulties in the latter are almost certainly due to Paul's emotional intensity at the time. That being so, some kind of periphrasis is the best hope of understanding it. For this reason the NEB should be consulted throughout. Though at times it is considerably fuller than the Greek, it reproduces the probable thought sequence well. Of the older translations, Moffatt is best.

6. Three times in short compass Paul will use the participle *hoi dokountes* (in various grammatical cases), meaning something like 'the influential men' (Arndt-Gingrich). But in each case the expression is slightly fuller and stronger, as though Paul's rising indignation is finding the studied courtesy of ii. 2 impossible to maintain. There, they are described as *hoi dokountes*, 'the somebodies'; by verse 6 they have become *hoi dokountes einai ti*, 'those who seemed to have some official position' (although Paul at once bursts out in indignant expostulation that God cares nothing about any such 'rating'). By verse 9, they are *hoi dokountes stuloi einai*, 'those who are rated as pillars of the church': and the veil of anonymity is dropped—they are Peter, James, and John. It is as though Paul deliberately refrains from giving them the disputed name of 'apostle' here (although he had done so in i. 17, where he had also included himself). To use it would have played into the hands of the Judaizers.

How much *whatsoever they were, hopoioi pote ēsan*, conceals is uncertain: it may mean only 'whatever you may like to call them', referring to this disliked title of apostle. It may, however, mean 'whatever they once were', referring to their peculiar position of favour during the earthly ministry of Christ to which they owed their present eminence. To Paul, this earthly knowledge of the Christ meant little compared with the transforming miracle of spiritual knowledge of the Messiah. To the Jewish Christian, on the other hand, such knowledge seems to have meant everything. Not only were the Twelve venerated as the earthly companions of Christ, His earthly brothers were apparently accorded a similar veneration. This was so much so that James, brother of the Lord, took the place of the martyred James, brother of John, without question. To Paul all of this would doubtless have been recognizing personal distinctions (NEB) which, by definition, is not the way that God works. It was because of this attitude that it was possible for a movement like that of the Judaizers to arise.

There is another word which, with variations, is used three times. It too gives a clue to the links in Paul's thought. i. 16 had said *ou prosanethemēn*, 'I did not consult with anyone'; ii. 2 had *anethemēn*, 'I laid before them (my gospel)'. Here in ii. 6 we have the defiant *emoi ouden prosanethento*, which AV translates *added nothing to me*. NEB mg. has 'gave me no further instructions'; NEB, 'did not prolong the consultation', is also possible. Paul has been asserting his independence throughout, not because he wants to claim an independent position for himself, but because he wants to prove the supernatural origin of both his gospel and his apostolate. To Paul, both stand or fall together.

7–9. The attitude of the orthodox Jewish-Christian church leaders to Paul is an interesting study for which there is, unfortunately, insufficient evidence in Scripture. The way in which he was hurried from place to place in the early days (Damascus, Jerusalem, Caesarea, Tarsus), usually as a result of the opposition that his fiery preaching stirred up, suggests that the leaders may have been somewhat embarrassed by the enthusiasm of this young convert. What Barnabas, perhaps his best friend among the Jerusalem group, had to face is clear both from Acts xv. 39 and this Epistle. Peter is treated summarily in ii. 11; and 2 Peter iii. 15, 16 shows what may be regarded as a very cautious attitude to 'our beloved brother Paul' that was doubtless characteristic of Peter in later days at least. Once bitten, twice shy. Acts xv shows a puzzled but loyal James accepting the palpable differences of approach and method in a kind of 'interim agreement'; but his real embarrassment is manifest in Acts xxi. 17-26. The irony of the situation is seen in the fact that it was this attempted compromise that, humanly speaking, caused Paul's arrest, imprisonment, and ultimate death, although to Paul this had a deeper explanation and meaning in the purposes of God.

Nevertheless, on this occasion, whether before the Council of Jerusalem, during the Council of Jerusalem, or at the close of the Council (for all three views are held), there was a full and glad recognition that there was only one gospel, shared alike by Jerusalem and Antioch. This sense of 'belongingness' was sealed by giving *the right hands of fellowship*. Clasped right hands were the sign of friendship and trust (see Arndt-Gingrich), and this action on the part of the church leaders in Jerusalem must have been a bitter blow to the Judaizers. The heavier blow was to follow. For if Paul's gospel was accepted, then his apostleship must be accepted too. Thus it was that the handclasp was also the seal on a bargain, they were 'accepted . . . as partners', as the NEB has it. By this action Paul's apostolate to the Gentiles was recognized as freely as Peter's to the Jews—the latter being an apostolate in which the other members of the College of Twelve shared apparently. They took this course not as a result of a complicated process of reasoning, but from observation of spiritual facts. Just as Peter's apostolic ministry to the Jews was sealed by the work of the Spirit in the hearts of the hearers (as in Acts i-v and ix. 31-42, for instance), so the seal of Paul's apostolic ministry was the harvest of the Gentiles given him by God. Paul had realized this all along, as we see from Acts xv. 3, 4. When he is approaching Jerusalem for the great tussle of the Council of Jerusalem he knows that his strongest argument is to report the conversion of the Gentiles. No man can gainsay that if he is honest spiritually. This was exactly the argument that the Lord had used when questioned either by puzzled believer or obstinate unbeliever. To close one's eyes to such spiritual evidence comes dangerously near to the sin against the Holy Spirit and neither James nor Peter were in danger of that. But perhaps the Judaizers were.

That this is the meaning of the passage is shown by the use of the verb *energeō*, 'to work within', and the noun *charis*, 'grace, spiritual gift', both associated with the work of the Holy Spirit in Paul and through Paul, as well as His work in and through Peter. Another irony of the passage (not lost entirely on Peter, if we consider Acts xv. 7) is that, in a sense, Peter's mantle had fallen on Paul, for it was Peter to whom had come in the first place the vision of the Gentile mission. Not only so, but it was the knowledge of the seal of the Spirit upon his work that had convinced Peter of the authentic nature of the call (Acts x. 47, xv. 8, 9). Later at Antioch, all his own arguments will be turned against him; but at Jerusalem there was no need. He himself used them stubbornly in the support of Paul.

Again, the attitude of the strictly orthodox Jews of Jerusalem would make an interesting study, were the materials a little richer. At best, they must have regarded Peter as a doubtful ally, especially after the Cornelius episode. This seems to mark a breach between him and the 'circumcision party' (Acts xi. 2, 3). After his bluff words at the Council (Acts xv. 7–11) they must have been even further estranged.

10. The Jerusalem *troika*, then, said nothing to Paul, *Only they would that we should remember the poor; the same which I also was forward* (RSV, 'eager') *to do*. Perhaps 'God's poor' or 'the *Poverini*' would be a better translation, for the reference is not to the general duty of almsgiving, binding on all good Jews in any case, but to the 'poor saints' of the Jerusalem church (so NEB, 'their poor'). There is no hint of this in Acts xv (although there is no reason why such an injunction should be included in the 'findings' of the Council), and the indignation expressed by Paul in the second half of the verse would be much more understandable if this were the 'famine relief' visit of Acts xi. It was, to say the least, unnecessary to invoke an 'Inter-Church-Aid Rescue Team' to remember the duty of mutual help: that was the whole purpose of their presence. *hoi ptōchoi, the poor*, is one of the early names for Christians which does not seem to be used outside Palestine. Others in the same class are Galilaeans (Acts ii. 7) or Nazarenes (Acts xxiv. 5). Early names like 'saints' (Acts ix. 32) or 'brothers' (Acts ix. 30) or 'disciples' (Acts ix. 26) continued to be used in the Gentile churches, even after the new name of 'Christian' was in use (Acts xi. 26). It seems a simple deduction that those names were still used which were felt to be still applicable. Naturally, 'Galilaeans' was inappropriate, and equally naturally 'the Poor' was inapplicable. It had a long history in Israel's literature, referring to the pious remnant of God's people. They were usually 'poor' in the economic sense of the word, and always 'poor' in the sense of being in special need of God's help (see Arndt-Gingrich on this word; for its Hebrew correspondences, see Abbott-Smith). No doubt the use of 'poor' and 'poor in spirit' in the Gospels had helped to make the word current in Christian as well as strictly Jewish circles. If the Christian Church was the new remnant, then the Christians were now 'God's poor'. Revelation ii. 9 and iii. 17 shows this metaphorical use still surviving. Paul himself makes use of the concept in passages like 2 Corinthians vi. 10 and viii. 9. But usually he introduces it in the context of Christian giving, not in the sense of James ii. 5, 6.

For the plain fact of the matter is that the Gentile churches might number many poor members in their midst, but there were also rich members. No Gentile church could be described as 'poor' in the sense of the grinding poverty of the Jerusalem church itself. The abuses of the Lord's Supper, mentioned in 1 Corinthians xi. 21, could take place only in churches where there was considerable inequality in the distribution of wealth. And this posits some wealth at least. But the greatest proof of the comparative wealth of the Gentile churches is that Paul did in fact manage to raise such a 'collection' for the Christians of Jerusalem. Indeed, it was one of the major concerns in all of his later Epistles, which are of a 'pastoral' nature.

There were doubtless various causes contributing to this chronic poverty of the churches in Judaea. Cynics will point to the experiment in communal living recorded in Acts iv. 34 as a possible cause. But we should notice two things even here: first, those who contributed large sums to this common 'pool' seem to have been 'Overseas Jews' (like Barnabas of Cyprus); secondly, the poverty of the church had far deeper roots if the bulk of the members were already poor. Palestine was at the time over-tilled and over-populated. Chronic rebellions and disturbances had worsened a position already made grave by the stony nature of the soil after more than a millennium of deforestation. Village India of today—and doubtless many other parts of the world—presents a picture not dissimilar. Added to this, the land was crowded with pilgrims returning to their home land for festivals. Jerusalem was a bloated religious capital, crammed with hungry, unproductive mouths. It seems to have had little true economic basis for its life.

espoudasa, translated by RSV 'I was eager to do', is ambiguous only in the interpretation of its tense. It may refer either to Paul's subsequent eagerness (NEB, 'I made it my business to do'), or past attitude (NEB mg. 'I had made it my business to do').

e. The clash with Peter (ii. 11–16)

Paul has now made clear that his attendance at Jerusalem was in no sense subservience to the apostles there. They had made no contribution to his position. But now he will go further in order to demonstrate the essential independence both of his gospel and of his position.¶

'When Cephas came to Antioch, I stood up to him, face to face, because he stood condemned. For before some parties came from James, he used to share meals with non-Jewish Christians; but as soon as they had come, he shrank back and made a clear break between himself and them—just because he was afraid of the "Circumcists". And the rest of the Jewish Christians joined him in acting this false role so that even Barnabas was actually carried away and did it along with them.

'So when I saw that they were not being straightforward about gospel truth, I said to Cephas in front of everybody, "If you, who start from a Jewish position, live like a non-Jew, and not a Jew, how can you try to force non-Jews to live like Jews?" We, who are Jews by birth, and thus not "sinful non-Jews", because we know that no man is justified by doing what the law commands, but only through trust in Christ Jesus— we ourselves have put our trust in Christ Jesus, with the aim of being justified as a result of our trust in Christ, and not as a result of our doing what the law commands (because "no man can be justified" by doing what the law commands).'

11. Unfortunately, we have no idea when Peter visited Antioch. If we translate *ēlthen* as 'had come' (which is just as likely), then he may have already been there for some considerable time when the recorded incident took place. In any case, for the charge of 'play-acting' to be effective Peter must have been there for a period long enough for men to observe that this Jerusalem Christian at least had no scruples about eating with Gentiles. All that is known is that Barnabas was also 'on the staff' of the church at Antioch at this time, and this would suggest an early period before the rift with Paul. But since we know almost nothing of the movements of Barnabas it is unwise to be dogmatic here. It is impossible to use the 'psychological argument', i.e. to say that it is inconceivable that Peter should have acted in this way after the recent conference with Paul (whether we consider it to have been the 'famine relief' visit, or the Council visit, or some other visit totally unrecorded in Acts). Another group of scholars will answer at once that, while it is, of course, possible that Paul narrates this episode out of its chronological order and that the event thus took place before the conference, we have no proof; nothing that Peter does is 'inconceivable'. If we protest that this makes Peter a weathercock, they will reply that this is precisely what Peter is—and that this is why Paul is so angry. Such circular arguments will take us nowhere.

Paul makes his point, that he 'stood up to', *antestēn*, Peter: but he wants to show that he had good reason for this. The man was *kategnōsmenos* (NEB, 'clearly in the wrong'); he was acting not only against his conscience and against the revelation that he had received in Acts x, but also against his whole past tradition and custom. Paul may have wanted at the same time to show that no Jerusalem church authority was infallible.

12. But it is not an honest mistake that stirs his wrath so much as the deceitfulness of it all. Peter's common practice at Antioch had been to 'mess' with the non-Jewish Christians; all knew that and all rejoiced. Peter at least was one to be trusted. He had been the first chosen by God to preach to Gentiles, as he either was yet to remind, or had already reminded, the Council of Jerusalem in Acts xv. No doubt, the church at Antioch had some common feeding arrangement for its members not unlike the 'community kitchen' of Jerusalem. If it did not extend to all members, it would certainly have covered those engaged in 'full-time ministry', for they would have had neither home to cook in nor means wherewith to buy food apart from the gifts of the Christians to whom they ministered.[1]

Thus *sunēsthien*, *he did eat with*, must have referred mainly to the common meal, which seems to have characterized the early Christian groups as surely as it did the Qumran community. But it cannot have failed to include the Lord's Supper. For if Peter ate with Christians on ordinary occasions, he surely joined with them in that final solemn moment at which they remembered the death of their common Lord. By the same rule, if Peter ceases to eat the common meals with them now, he also ceases to join them at the Lord's Table. How narrow the line of demarcation was between the 'church feast' and the Lord's Supper we can see from the very possibility of Corinthian abuses arising at all. In the modern 'abstract' setting, such things are unthinkable. So Peter is refusing to sit at the Lord's Table with fellow-Christians. Worse still, this is not

---

[1] Although Paul often worked for his own living, he seems to have regarded this as a special case, not to be generalized as far as 'seniors' of the church are concerned (see 1 Tim. v. 18). But 1 Corinthians ix. 4, 5 shows us that Paul realized very well that neither Peter, nor the Jerusalem apostles, nor the Lord's brothers, had any of his scruples about accepting local church support.

from conscience, but because he fears *them which were of the circumcision.*

Who were these 'certain men' who came from James? Again, it sounds as if Paul is preserving a studied anonymity; he could perhaps give names if he so desired. This is the more likely if, with NEB mg., we adopt the other possible reading and translate, 'a certain person'. The words 'from James' are not as strong in Greek as in English, but they express controlled indignation. Paul is not implying that James of necessity sent them (indeed, James denies this in Acts xv. 24); but they were certainly men from James's circle, James's group, the Jerusalem church. The implied criticism is that James should not have tolerated such views. James in Acts xv. 24 does accept full responsibility for them being of his circle (using the same preposition *apo*, 'from') but denies that he gave them any commission to spread their views among the Gentiles. They were clearly his own 'right wing', the Pharisaic group, and a sore embarrassment even to him. We give much thought to the problems of Paul, but few to those of James. This is scarcely equitable, especially in view of the vast range of opinion among Jewish Christendom. Paul describes this group, here and elsewhere, as *hoi ek peritomēs*, often translated 'the circumcision party'. In our paraphrase above, it has been translated 'the Circumcists', as descriptive of their distinctive practice. The word might, however, mean no more than 'the circumcised', i.e. 'the Jews'; or, at a deeper level, 'those from the Jewish Church', using *peritomē* as a collective term for Jewish Christendom. Why Peter should be afraid of this group of extremists in Antioch, when he is prepared to beard them in Jerusalem, is a problem that we cannot explain without remembering our own psychological 'kinks'. Of course, if this happened before the Council, perhaps Peter learned his lesson on this occasion.

13. Had this piece of 'play-acting', this playing false to his own convictions, ended with Peter, it might not have been so serious. But all the rest of the (local) Jewish Christians were carried away by the tide—including even faithful Barnabas.

Paul had to act quickly, or there would be 'two communions' in Antioch, two Christian groups existing side by side but unwilling to share the Lord's Supper together. This was unthinkable to Paul, although today we accept it as a matter of course. When we attempt to estimate the character of Barnabas, we should not forget this incident. It shows the danger of theological compromise, the besetting sin of loving natures. To Barnabas, no doubt, this was simply a matter of love. He did not want to grieve the brethren from Jerusalem; a brief abstention from fellowship with his Gentile fellow-believers was all that would be necessary. Once the Jerusalem emissaries had departed the old terms could be resumed. Was not this a small sacrifice to make for peace? But to Paul, this was 'peace at any price', and he was not prepared to buy peace on those terms.

We can see here all the elements that led to the breach between Barnabas and Paul on the question of John Mark (Acts xv. 39). It is not our responsibility to judge between rights and wrongs there, especially in a context where the Scripture refrains from so doing. Some have held that John Mark's final reinstatement is the proof that Paul was mistaken (see 2 Tim. iv. 11). But in this case at Antioch there can be no doubt but that Paul was right in his stand. And he knows it. The one anomaly is that, had not Barnabas been what he was, there might well have been no Paul to withstand him; for, under God, Paul owed to Barnabas both his introduction to the Christian circle at Jerusalem and, later, to the Christian ministry at Antioch (Acts ix. 27, xi. 25f.). But Paul was too faithful a friend to allow him to go unrebuked.

14. The word *orthopodousin* has occasioned much discussion. True, it may mean 'act straightforwardly', as translated above: but the NEB mg. translation, 'making progress', is equally possible. We should then take the whole phrase as 'not advancing in the direction of the truth of the gospel'.[1] The main sense is clear, however.

[1] See Arndt-Gingrich with references to several valuable papers and articles on the subject. Note especially Kilpatrick's rendering 'they were not on the right road toward the truth of the gospel'.

Paul lays stress on the fact that, while his earlier talks with Peter and James at Jerusalem had been *kat' idian*, 'in private' (ii. 2), this rebuke was *emprosthen pantōn, before them all*. Peter's feelings are not recorded, but they can be imagined; his trick was all in vain. Everybody in the local church at Antioch knew very well that Peter was in the habit of living *ethnikōs*, 'like a non-Jew'. Probably the main reference is to the complicated system of Jewish food-laws which made social intercourse between Jew and Gentile almost impossible. This was indeed Peter's strong point; he had received a special revelation and its validity had been accepted by some of the Jerusalem church (see Acts xi, though the final reaction of the Pharisaic party is not recorded): Peter gained nothing by the deception. Even the very Judaizers must have known his past lapse in this area; and if they did not, there would doubtless have been local church members glad to tell them in hushed tones. But in what way was he trying to compel *the Gentiles to live as do the Jews*? No doubt Peter would have rightly protested that nothing was further from his thoughts. But this was precisely the aim of the Judaizers, and this was their purpose in coming to Antioch. Peter's ambiguous behaviour was playing right into their hands and Paul wants to shock him into seeing this clearly.

There may be another reason. Peter would not realize it, but this withdrawal from fellowship with Gentile Christians was tantamount to saying that they were not as good as Jewish Christians and that in some way they lacked something of the fullness of the gospel. Otherwise, why separate? The Judaizers would have admitted this at once. If Peter were pressed, he would no doubt deny it. But the action of both Peter and the Judaizers asserted it (for we can be sure that the Judaizers would not join with Gentiles at Antioch at meals of any kind), and it was their action that counted. When we refuse to eat at the Lord's Table with one whom we yet acknowledge to be a fellow-Christian, it can only be because we consider ourselves to have something that he has not—whether it be a mode of baptism, or some theory of apostolic succession, or some particular theological doctrine. This in effect denies to him the full status of Christian, and, to Paul, that depends solely on his relationship to Christ by faith. Of course, the Judaizers went far beyond Peter. They would have the Gentiles actually circumcised, and keep not only food laws, but the whole law of Moses. Paul will deal with this in the next section of his letter.

From verse 15 to the end of the chapter, there follows a passage of close theological argument, in many ways anticipating chapters iii and iv. As we try to interpret it we face the kind of problem which meets us so often in John's Gospel. Where do Paul's words to Peter on this historic occasion come to an end, and where does his theological reflection for the benefit of the Galatians begin? Probably the answer is that he passes from one to the other easily, without being conscious of the change himself. The opening verses certainly make better sense if we imagine them as part of an expostulation addressed nominally to Peter, but actually to all the Jewish Christians present, whether members of the local church or strangers from Jerusalem. The argument is strictly Jewish; for the moment the Gentile Christians, whether of Antioch or Galatia, have become awed onlookers at a battle of Titans.

15. *We who are Jews by nature.* Paul starts with the known position of the Jewish Christian, making for the purposes of argument no distinction between Judaizer and himself. He had already made it painfully clear that he sees no distinction between the Judaizer and Peter. But here he makes no distinction because there is no distinction. They had all alike believed in Christ with a view to being saved. That in itself is a confession that the old system of Judaism was not enough. If keeping the law had been a way to win acceptance with God, then there would have been no need for Christ to have come. He accepts the fact that they are *not sinners of the Gentiles* or 'Gentile dogs'. (The word *hamartōloi* probably applies more to shamelessness than to anything else; Paul is of course using, somewhat bitterly, the common terms within Judaism.) By this he means that they were presumably free from the grosser

vices of those around them, those vices which were directly
restrained by the law of Moses.

16. Nevertheless, by believing in Jesus as Messiah, the
Jewish Christians had shown that they knew that *a man is not
justified by the works of the law.* For Christ had made it clear that
He had no message of salvation for 'the righteous', but only
for those who were conscious of their status as 'sinners' (Mt.
ix. 13). All Jewish Christians, therefore, had initially agreed
that it was utterly impossible to commend themselves to God
by law-keeping. They had shown it by abandoning law-
observance as a possible means of salvation, and turning
instead to that offered freely by the Messiah. At the end of
verse 16 this position is reinforced, suitably enough, by a
reference to Psalm cxliii. 2. Now, all Paul has to do is to
show that the present insistence of the Judaizers on the keeping
of the law is utterly at variance with their own basic attitude.
It is not only Peter who is playing false to his own deepest
convictions; all of them are doing it.

f. Death and the new life (ii. 17–21)

'But if, at the very moment when we are desiring to be justified
through Christ, we prove to be sinners ourselves, does that
mean that Christ is only causing us to sin? Perish the very
thought. I say this because, if I try to build up again what I
once pulled down, I only prove myself to be a law-breaker.
For I, through law, "died" as far as law was concerned—so
that I might "live" as far as God is concerned.

'I shared Christ's cross. It is no longer I that live, but Christ
lives in me. I live my present earthly life in commitment to
God's Son, the One who loved me, and surrendered Himself
for me. No, I am not going to declare God's gracious act
invalid: I say this, because, if righteousness comes through the
law, then after all Christ died to no purpose.'

17. The passage 17–19 is again not easy to interpret. Here
the problem is not disjointed thought and language but some
ambiguities in the first sentence. The question centres on the

exact meaning of *heurethēmen hamartōloi*, translated above 'we prove to be sinners'. In view of the later development of the argument, NEB mg. is probably right with 'we no less than the Gentiles have accepted the position of sinners'. In either case, *hamartōloi* is to be understood with reference to our position in the eyes of God rather than our direct moral condition (although it is the same used above for 'Gentile sinners'; this can hardly be an accident as a different word is used below). Those who have thought that the word referred to actual sin see a direct reference to the Judaizing charge that Paul preached 'antinomianism'. To the Jew his gospel of salvation by grace through faith in Christ would remove all incentive for moral effort. In their eyes it would lead to a lower moral standard than under the law of Moses. Therefore, even Christ would have only become *hamartias diakonos*, 'a minister of sin', or 'abettor of sin' (NEB). Paul recoils from such a blasphemy with horror. As often, his first reaction is not theological argument; but a strong sense that this is utterly inconsistent with the revealed nature of God. There is no need to show in detail how utterly false such a charge would be. In the third and last section of the letter (the Moral Argument) Paul will develop this thought.

If the first sentence had been standing by itself, unquestionably this would have been the simplest interpretation. But in view of what follows, it is better to understand it something after the following: 'If, at the very moment while we say that we ourselves are justified by faith alone, we turn out to be preaching to others that "faith alone" is inadequate, but that they must keep the law as well, does that not mean that trusting in Christ is only leading them into sin? for it is teaching them not to trust the law.'

The exact meaning of *dikaioumai*, translated conventionally 'to be justified', need not be discussed in detail, since the dispute is not over what it is, but how it is to be obtained. In general terms it means to be put in right relation with God. Arndt-Gingrich therefore translate it, 'to be acquitted, be pronounced and treated as righteous, and thereby become *dikaios* (righteous), receive the divine gift of *dikaiosunē* (righteousness).' This reflects the modern swing from a purely forensic understanding of the verb (which could, at extremes, resemble a legal fiction) to a realization that it is fundamentally a 'salvation-word', closely connected with the biblical concept of grace. Without obliterating the biblical distinction between justification and sanctification, it is important to realize that being 'put right' with God involves a subsequent total change in our moral behaviour (though this in itself could never commend us to God).

18. This verse is plain sailing, especially if the interpretation of verse 17 is correct. The Judaizers, with their reintroduction of law-keeping as an essential of salvation, are painfully rebuilding the very structure of human 'merit' that, for Paul, had come crashing in ruins on the Damascus road. At best all I can do through the law is to show that I am a *parabatēs*, a 'law-breaker'. Paul will explain elsewhere that this is the whole function of the law of Moses. But there is no path to salvation lying in that direction.

19. For Paul, the 'once-for-allness' of his conversion experience will allow no return. Perhaps he remembers those three days of darkness and agony of mind in Straight Street before Ananias came and the light streamed in. The law had brought him to the gates of death; he was in despair, a condemned criminal, with no hope. So be it; he accepted 'death' as far as the law was concerned. He would never again turn to it, hoping for a path of life. But he turned from it as a way of self-commendation to God only in order to find the path of life offered by God in Christ.

20. Calmer water has been reached now. Paul will try to explain more clearly this spiritual experience of his that has involved a revulsion from the law (to which he had after all devoted the best years of his life). The Jew could think of a Rabbi wedded to the Torah in much the same way as a mediaeval churchman might regard a bishop as wedded to the Church. What unfaithfulness is this to leave Torah and seek a new bride? Elsewhere, Paul will use this 'marriage' metaphor with effect (see Rom. vii. 3). Here, although Galatians is in many respects the 'rough draft' of Romans, he does not actually use the analogy. But the psychological problem is still the same. How can he explain this change, this revulsion?

In many ways, this is one of the central passages of Galatians. It is, indeed, a text frequently used by preachers, but it is important to realize that it is not so much an exhortation to personal sanctification as a powerful argument for the total sufficiency and efficacy of the work of Christ. It is true that it deals with the great motives for Christian service, but the central thought is the complete breach with the old ways of thought that is demanded by faith-committal to Christ. The 'faith that justifies' is total, in extent if not in quantity.

But what does he mean when he says *I am crucified with Christ*, or better 'I have been crucified with Christ' (NEB, giving the sense of past action issuing in abiding result)? Again, the context does not justify us in seeing an account of a mystical experience. There are references to such in Paul's writings (see 2 Cor. xii. 2), but this is not one. This is a simple statement of Paul's relation to the law. It stands for a complete change in his way of looking at all things—a 'reorientation of thought', to use the modern jargon. He means that, as the death of Christ marked a total change in the relationship of Christ to all things (*imprimis*, to the law of Moses—or even law, as a principle, in the wider sense) so it did for Paul. The cross was, for Christ, a complete break with this life. In one sense every human death is such a break, although there was a deeper sense in which it was true of Christ. He had perfectly fulfilled the law; we have utterly failed. But for both law is now no more. Henceforth, Paul is dead to all claims of the law to be able to commend him to God. Such appeals fail to arouse him. He has long ago plumbed that agony and has reached the freedom on the other side. Men who spend all their lives in fear of death sometimes find a strange relief when death itself comes; there is nothing left to fear. So it was with Paul; he had laboured all his life under the nagging fear that perhaps in spite of all his rigorous observance of the law, he might not be able after all to win God's favour thus. Now, as he sees the cross of Christ, and realizes all the work of love and grace that was necessary to save him, he freely admits that this nagging fear was justified. Not only is it possible that he may fail to commend himself to God; it is actually impossible for him so to do. There go all his hopes. A lifetime of accumulation of 'merit' is wasted. He must confess himself a sinner like any Gentile. That is the death of the 'old man', the last killing blow to pride and self-esteem. There Paul dies—and who shall assess the agony of that death for the proud self-righteous Pharisee? But likewise, who can tell the blessed peace and relief that has come now that the old suppressed fear has been faced and acknowledged, or the new freedom and joy that comes from such release? We do well not to explain a spiritual experience in psychological terms alone. Yet some under-standing of our own psychological 'make-up' will help us to enter into Paul's thought here. If we do enter into it, we shall understand that a return to the law, seen as a possible means of 'putting himself in the right' in God's eyes, is an utter impossibility to Paul.

It is not Paul's way to sketch the negative side alone, though sometimes, as here, the exigencies of controversy may demand that he deals with the negative side of the question first. At once he moves on to the positive aspect, to describe the new release of spiritual life and power. *Nevertheless I live*. Live? Of course he lives—but it is Christ living in him now. As in the old days the law had filled his horizon and dominated his thought-life, so now it is Christ. Christ is the sole meaning of life for him now; every moment is passed in conscious depen-dence on Him, to whom he looks for everything. This is Christian faith; and it is intensely personal, both as regards subject and object, if these terms are allowed. It is faith in God's Son (linking the cross with the will of the Father) *who loved* Paul, and *gave himself* (NEB, 'sacrificed himself') for Paul.

21. After this impassioned outburst, verse 21 is a calmer summary. An attitude like that of Paul's is a full appreciation of the grace of God shown in Christ. But to act like the Judaizers is to declare this grace invalid (RSV, NEB, 'nullify').

Obviously this is so. If they are preaching a return to law-keeping, it can only be because they consider what God did on the cross as being ineffectual. Furthermore, if this is true, *then Christ is dead in vain,* His death was gratuitous; it achieved nothing. He might as well not have died. The reason and sheer logic of this is incontrovertible.

II. THE ARGUMENT FROM THEOLOGY (iii. i–v. 1)

Paul could well have closed his Epistle at the end of chapter ii. The storm has passed into a calm and his point has been made. But, as he thinks of what has happened in Galatia, his feelings overwhelm him as they did in i. 6, and he returns to the charge for the second time. So it is that chapter iii will introduce a whole new section of his argument, that from theology or, more exactly, from Scripture. This may either be because it was natural to a Jew, particularly one with Paul's rabbinic training, to turn to the Scriptures for proof in any argument. Or it may be because he knows that his Judaizing opponents will already have made great play of the Scriptures to prove their case. Whatever the reason, it will not surprise us if Paul's use of the Old Testament Scriptures is, at times, more 'rabbinic' than we would find natural. Both his own background and the nature of his opponents' training make this inevitable. But such a 'rabbinic approach' extends only to the manner of citing and treating the Scriptures, not to the Scriptures themselves. And we shall find that the great theological principles to which Paul appeals are as valid today as in first-century Galatia, although we might express them in different terminology. Much study has recently been devoted to Paul's rabbinic background, and its possible influence on his exegesis, if not his theology. Davies, Daube, Schoeps and Munck may be mentioned as being particularly helpful[1].

Hitherto, Paul has argued from his own spiritual experience, and the facts of Christian history. Now he will show that such experience is not subjective and illusory, but grounded upon

[1] For the full titles of their works see the List of Abbreviations, p. 9.

the eternal purposes of God as revealed in His Word. But before he does that, in a short opening section, he will appeal briefly to the spiritual experience of the very Galatians to whom he writes and link it to the similar experience of Abraham. This has a twofold object. First, Paul wishes to show the Galatians that their present attitude is a contradiction not only of his spiritual history, but also of their own (for Paul's spiritual pilgrimage is not reserved for 'princes of the church'; it is and should be normative for every Christian, however humble). Secondly, he wants to show them that this common pilgrimage, both his and theirs, was also that of Abraham; otherwise, to quote the example of Abraham to the Galatians would be utterly irrelevant. As it is, we find with a shock that Abraham's problems are our problems, even though the outward circumstances are so dissimilar. From that, we shall move to the point where we see that Abraham's solution can be our solution, since Abraham's God is our God.

Paul has another crowning argument that he will use later. Abraham himself is, in one sense, a Gentile like the Galatians. He is no Jew, though he became the ancestor of the Jews. He knew nothing of the law of Moses, nothing of the Temple, nothing of later food laws, nothing of circumcision itself, in early days at least. He was not ancestor of the Jews alone: all the desert peoples of the Negev, the 'Southland', traced their ancestry to him. Moreover, in God's gracious promise to him, Gentiles found special mention. Judaizers might quote Moses; Paul will quote Abraham. Let them quote law; he will quote promise. If they appeal to centuries of tradition and the proud history of the law of Moses, he will appeal to the grander 'covenant with Abraham', older by centuries still.

While Paul will pursue these arguments at greater length in Romans, they are present in all their strength in Galatians. Indeed, one of the most striking proofs that Paul was not lying in what he said in earlier chapters as to his gospel being independent of outside (especially Jerusalem) influences is not only that his gospel is so distinctive, but also that it shows no sign of 'development' over the years. No doubt this was the way in which Paul had come to terms with himself and with the Old Testament during those early days in Arabia.

a. Introduction (iii. 1-6)

'You stupid Galatians, who hoodwinked you? The message of Jesus as Messiah who died on the cross was plastered up on the bill-boards before your very eyes. This is the one thing that I want to find out from you. Did you receive the Spirit by doing what the law demands or by believing the message that you heard? Can you be as stupid as that? Are you trying to finish by natural means some process that began supernaturally? Have you been through so much, and all for nothing?—that is, if it should turn out to be all for nothing. God is continually providing you with the Spirit as a free gift and continually working deeds of power among you. Does He do it because you do what the law bids or because you believe the message that you hear? That was just Abraham's case; he believed God, and his belief was regarded as righteousness.'

1. Again, a paraphrase of the whole passage is the best introduction to a commentary upon it, for all through this central part of Galatians the interpretation of the part depends on the interpretation of the whole. Paul does not accuse the Galatians of desperate sin, he does accuse them of being *anoētoi, foolish*, 'stupid'. After the Second World War a group of German pastors were lamenting that they had been misled by 'daemonic forces' when a senior pastor present brought things from near hysteria to sober realization of the fact by saying drily: 'Gentlemen, we have all been very foolish.' Paul never denies the reality of the spiritual battle for the souls of men. No man believes more firmly than he in the existence and operation of 'daemonic forces' (see, e.g., Eph. vi. 12). But he will not have the Galatians shift the blame from themselves. A sheer lack of logical reasoning has led them into this inconsistency. As we read Paul's close argument it seems so simple and obvious that we wonder why we never saw it so before. But that is the mark of Paul the trained theologian as well as the man filled by the Spirit. Paul never condemns the human intellect as such. In fallen man, it shares the fall; it must be brought under Christ's rule, like every other part (see 2 Cor. x. 5). After that, Paul is as anxious as any that we should serve God with our intellect as well as 'spiritually' (see 1 Cor. xiv. 14 ff.). While it is true that spiritual things are spiritually discerned, it is equally true (to enlarge a famous definition) that theology is nothing more than the ordinary rules of grammar and logic applied to the text of Scripture.

Some scholars have seen significance in the use of the word *Galatians* here as having bearing on the geographic destination of the letter. It was addressed, in i. 2, to 'the Christian congregations of Galatia'. Most have felt that this must refer to an area, possibly an administrative area, but that it gives no clue as to race and therefore no clue as to whether the recipients were the Celtic tribes of the north or the mixed population of the southern cities. But if Paul actually describes them as 'Galatians', does this not prove that they are Galatians by race? If so, they must have been the Celtic folk on the northern plateau. But if Paul could call the whole area 'Galatia' (as he seems to do), then there is no *a priori* reason why he should not have called the inhabitants 'Galatians', whether or no they would be pleased by such a term.

It is most unlikely that Paul is using the word as a term of abuse, as though he were saying 'You foolish country bumpkins', though it is true that in Hellenistic literature the *Galatai* are described as *aphrōnes*, another word for 'stupid'. Paul may abuse his Judaizing enemies roundly. He is hardly likely to be directly insulting to his own converts, especially as he is trying to get them to see his point. Similarly, it would be foolish to try to settle the destination of the letter by examining the assumed 'racial characteristics' of the Celts, and comparing them with the known situation in Galatia. Luther thought, from this reasoning, that the Galatians were Germans; most modern German commentators have felt that they were French, not always with French agreement. The Irish are also notably sensitive on the matter. Perhaps the best interpretation is to say that the Galatians are everyman; fickleness of this type is part of human nature. That, indeed, is why the Epistle is universally applicable; it speaks to all men everywhere at all times. Otherwise, it would be a mere historical document, of archaeological interest only.

But Paul does not lay all the blame on the Galatians, whoever they were. *Who hath bewitched you?* he asks. The word *ebaskanen* is the same root as the English 'fascinated'. We can imagine the fascination with which these simple Christians must have listened to the glib tongues from Jerusalem. But Paul will not waste time on the deceivers; they must give account before God, who alone can judge the hearts (1 Cor. iv. 5). Some have felt that the singular *tis, who*, supports the reading of the singular in ii. 12. In that case this would refer to the arch-Judaizer, whoever he is. They would also say that this verse proves Paul's ignorance of his identity. But this is not necessarily so. The stress is more on *bewitched*. Paul is not really interested in the idle question as to who the man is. After such a clear presentation of the gospel they must surely have been bewitched to forget its one salient point so soon. This in itself shows that the alternative possible translation, 'Who envied you?', is unlikely. Perhaps the Judaizers did secretly envy the Galatians their Christian freedom, but that is not the point here.

The Galatians are men 'before whose eyes Jesus Christ was openly displayed upon his cross' (NEB). Presumably this refers to the content of the preaching of Paul during their initial evangelism. 1 Corinthians ii. 2 shows us that total domination of all Pauline theology by the fact of the cross was no accident; it came of deliberate and set purpose of mind. The word *proegraphē*, 'was displayed', may mean either 'portrayed' or 'placarded publicly', like some notice of civic interest. The huge hoardings that carry advertisements by roadsides would be the best parallel in our modern world. There is no missing such an announcement. For the other possible translation 'set forth in a public proclamation', see Arndt-Gingrich. This would be a more direct reference to Paul's public preaching. It is a New Testament commonplace to see the preacher as God's herald, God's town-crier (see 1 Tim. ii. 7 (NEB), though the verb is far more common than the noun).

The word *estaurōmenos*, *crucified*, is interesting from its tense; it is the perfect passive participle which usually expresses a continuing result. So NEB translates 'upon his cross'; so we might render it 'Jesus, a crucified Messiah'. That one phrase cuts the ground from under all Judaizers, if only they understood it; and yet it is thoroughly Jewish in every word.

2. One simple question will now be enough to convict the Galatians of the folly of their attitude. How did their Christian life begin? Or, as Paul puts it here: *Received ye the Spirit by the works of the law?* No: clearly the Spirit is not something to be won by striving to obey the law's demands; it is God's free gift. Then how was the Spirit received? By hearing the good news of, *inter alia*, the gift of the Spirit, and by accepting the gift in simple faith; that is, *by the hearing of faith*, by hearing and believing. Of course, they knew that this was just as true for them as for Paul. It was equally true of the very Judaizers, if they were Christians at all; but Paul is not addressing them here.

There are several possible translations of the phrase *ex akoēs pisteōs*, paraphrased by NEB as 'by believing the gospel message': NEB mg. suggests either 'by the message of faith' or 'by hearing and believing'. The last of these seems the best, but the difference is not great in any case. The opposition is to *ex ergōn nomou*, *by the works of the law*, which means 'keeping the law' (NEB). To Paul, 'hearing' is very important: faith comes by hearing—that is why to preach God's word is so essential (Rom. x. 14–17). For the importance of hearing about the Spirit so that we may enjoy the gift of the Spirit we might perhaps compare the puzzled 'Spirit-less' disciples of Ephesus (Acts xix. 1–7). There is no suggestion here that any laying-on of hands had anything to do with the gift of the Spirit; it is associated directly with belief in the gospel and the response of faith. After the early chapters of Acts, we have no sure reference associating the gift with such an outward rite (for it is not certain whether 1 Tim. iv. 14 refers to 'confirmation' or 'ordination', to use modern terms which may not be wholly appropriate). Even in Acts, the coming of the Spirit sometimes antedated the laying-on of hands, as in Acts x. 44 where it even antedates baptism. It seems, therefore, better to regard the rite in those days as having an evidential value. Whether or no Paul continued it in the churches which he founded, we cannot say. In any case, as he was not one of the Twelve, the Jerusalem group would no doubt have regarded such 'confirmations' as highly irregular.

3. Paul often contrasts the beginning and end of a process; here, he uses the contrasting pair of words *pneumati* and *sarki*, *Spirit* and *flesh*. It would be impossible in a book of this size to examine the full meaning of either word.[1] It is the less necessary to discuss them here (see under Galatians iv) as they do not carry any great theological weight in this context except as a pair of opposites, corresponding to the alternatives open to the Galatians after such a gospelling as they had had. Fairly enough, therefore, NEB translates 'the spiritual' and 'the material'. There is, of course, a slight play on words in that the Christian life of the Galatians has indeed begun 'by the reception of the Spirit'. What Paul means is that the whole Christian way is 'supernatural' from start to finish; but the Jewish path (whatever it might have been in design and origin) has become a thoroughly 'naturalistic' way. Every 'heathen' in every religion is trying to earn his own salvation, as the Jews are; the only difference is that the pagan has not such clear knowledge. From this angle Judaism is just 'another religion'; although, from another angle, it has an eternal value as God's preparation for the gospel of Christ.

4. There is a slight ambiguity in the *tosauta epathete*: it might mean *Have ye suffered so many things?* as in AV, in which case it would refer to the persecutions that the Galatians had suffered from their fellow-countrymen. If they are the inhabitants of the south of Galatia then we have sufficient evidence in Acts xiv of the sort of treatment that the converts may have received, both from Jews and from the local countryfolk.

But probably the meaning is simply 'Have you had such wonderful spiritual experiences all to no purpose?' (cf. NEB).

[1] There is a full discussion in Arndt-Gingrich, with good book-lists.

This would fit the context better, with its references to the gift of the Spirit and the subsequent miraculous manifestations. Again, Acts xiv. 10 would be an example if the churches were in the South Galatia region; but doubtless there were many unrecorded instances of similar happenings. Paul is loath even to admit the possibility of such experiences being *in vain*. But if the Galatians slip back into the twilight of a half-Jewish faith, it will mean not only the end of all such manifestations of the Spirit; it will mean that they might as well never have had the experience for all the good that it did them. Christ would have died to no purpose; the Spirit would have been given to no purpose also.

5. The word used for the giving of the Spirit, *epichorēgōn*, has an interesting history in Classical Greek: by Hellenistic days, however, its main two fields of meaning are either 'give', 'grant freely', or 'support', 'help' (see Arndt-Gingrich). Either of these would suit to describe the gift of the Paraclete to the Christian.

6. Having already linked the experience of the Galatians with his own, in a final flourish (which will introduce the main matter of the section) Paul links it to the experience of Abraham. 'Why, that is exactly what Abraham did', he says. Abraham, like the Galatians, had *believed God*, trusted God's word—and God accepted that faith, that trust, as though it were that 'right standing with God' which Abraham manifestly could never win by his own efforts, *it was accounted to him for righteousness*. In other words, Abraham entered into his particular blessing by realizing that he could do nothing himself, confessing it to God, and throwing himself on God, counting on God to do what he could not. That is the paradox of faith, as true for us as for Abraham. It was by ceasing to try to do anything for himself, and by accepting this position of humble and utter dependence, that Abraham was 'justified'. Nor was this a 'legal fiction'. This attitude alone is 'right standing' with God, for any other attitude is stubborn pride and self-righteousness.

b. Abraham's faith (iii. 7-9)

Having laid down his basic principle, Paul now needs to show the Galatians that Abraham has something to do with them, and this he does by close exegesis of the Genesis texts. One wonders whether his Gentile converts were as familiar with the Old Testament as Paul was. But in South Galatia at least there had been considerable Jewish settlements (as the presence of the half-Jew Timothy shows), and we may perhaps assume a considerable Jewish and proselyte element in the church. In any case, whether they knew it or not, the Old Testament and the Old Testament alone was the Bible of the New Testament Church. If they used 'texts', it was from there that the preachers chose them, adding no doubt words, sayings, and remembered incidents from the life of Jesus to show how He fulfilled these Scriptures. Besides, as already noted, it was from these Scriptures that the Judaizers reasoned. This, therefore, must be the battleground.

'I suppose you realize that those who have faith are Abraham's descendants. For the Scripture, foreseeing that God is One who justifies the Gentiles as a result of their trust, preached the gospel in advance to Abraham when it said, "All the Gentiles will be blessed through you". So then those who believe do enjoy blessing along with believing Abraham.'

7. Modern scholars often lose patience with what they describe as 'rabbinic' exegesis, but a little patience will nearly always show the relevant theological principles. Here there is nothing forced, and no difficulty. Perhaps *hoi ek pisteōs* should be translated 'the faith party', as opposed to *hoi ek peritomēs*, 'the circumcision party' in ii. 12. RSV and NEB are neutral with 'men of faith'. In any case it clearly means those who, like Abraham, are trusting to God to do what they have given up trying to do for themselves, namely, commend themselves to God as worthy. Such men, says Paul, are *the children of Abraham*; they bear the family likeness in the shape of this faith. From the Gospels we know that this is an argument that the Lord Himself had used as, for example, in John viii. 33-44. It is possible that Paul knew of the tradition of this conversation. It is always possible that we should translate *huioi Abraam*, not so much *children* (or 'sons') *of Abraham* as 'real Abrahams'. This would be following the normal Semitic practice by which, for instance, wicked men are called 'sons of Belial'. But as, in the case of Abraham, physical descent was regularly stressed by the Jews, and spiritual descent by Paul, it seems more appropriate to hold to the traditional translation.

8. When Paul says 'Scripture says', or as here, *Scripture, foreseeing*, he is not crediting the Bible with an existence independent of God; he is simply using a normal Jewish form of speech. For him, 'Scripture says' is the equivalent of saying 'The Lord of Scripture says'. Here, therefore, his meaning is that the wording of Scripture is appropriate and corresponds to what God does in the gospel of Christ. Nor is this, to Paul, an accident; it is the deliberate control by God of the content of Scripture. Any study of the Pauline doctrine of inspiration and revelation must take this into account.

The word *dikaioi*, 'justifies', is probably not to be taken in the old way, 'would yet, in the future, justify', although it is true that, in the New Testament, the present tense frequently has a future meaning (rather as we say, 'Tomorrow I am going away'). It is better to see in it a continuous present. God is 'the Gentile-Justifier', the One whose way it is ever to justify the Gentiles purely on the ground of their faith, their helpless committal to Him in trust. Indeed, this is what God was doing at that very moment in the case of Abraham. The only difference now is that the reason for the possibility of such a process is suddenly made plain in Jesus Christ.

This also helps to explain *proeuēngelisato*, 'preached the gospel beforehand' ('Scripture' being the formal subject, but God the actual subject). In one sense, no Christian could speak of the gospel being preached before Calvary. In another, here is an anticipation of it. Indeed, it is more than an anticipation in that God's ways of dealing with men are eternally the same. For the turn of speech, we may compare John viii. 56, where Christ speaks of Abraham having seen His day. It was a commonplace of Jewish thought that Abraham was a prophet (Gn. xx. 7). The exact meaning of the Hebrew behind *eneulogēthēsontai* is disputed. It might be translated 'bless themselves' rather than *be blessed*. In that case it would mean that, when Gentiles wished to invoke blessing on one another, they would say, 'May the God of Abraham bless you', because they could conceive of no higher blessing to use. Genesis xviii. 18 should probably be translated thus, whatever may be the case with Genesis xii. 3 (see RSV). But the traditional Jewish exegesis was the straight passive, and the ultimate difference not great. Paul clearly takes it as a direct passive here.

9. He can now round off the passage triumphantly by showing that, as a plain matter of fact, the 'faith-men' are indeed at this moment enjoying the blessing of God, just as much as trusty Abraham. *pistō* is clearly active in sense meaning 'believing', rather than the passive 'trusted'. The Roman Catholic use of the word 'the faithful', as applied to their church members, preserves this sense.

c. Who is under the curse? (iii. 10–14)

Paul must now swing at once to meet a flank attack, real or expected. The Judaizers will have been fuming with impatience all this time. Why talk about Abraham when the real question is the law? Abraham stood at the very beginning of God's revelatory process. Centuries later God crowned the process by giving the law of Moses. It is by keeping this law that Israel looks for salvation. If God in His mercy used some other system with Abraham, that was because there was as yet no law to keep. Indeed, the Rabbis wasted much ingenuity in trying to prove that the patriarchs had in fact kept the law, though it had not yet been revealed. That was necessary to maintain the respectability of Abraham, not to uphold the cohesiveness of their own self-contained system. What the Judaizers were preaching to the Galatians was the utter necessity of law-keeping (in part at least) as a *sine qua non* of salvation. To them all this talk about Abraham was irrelevant to the main issue.

The common opinion of the Jewish scholar was that the

vulgar *am haaretz*, the common folk who had neither knowledge of, nor interest in, the law, were under God's curse (see John vii. 49, which could be paralleled by much stronger language outside the Bible). Here Paul turns the tables; it is the Jewish scholar, not the Gentile sinner, who is clearly under 'the (celebrated) curse'. The details of the meaning of this will be given below. At the moment, the sole question is the curse's *locus*, and Paul is clear on that question. Verses 10 and 11 may be paraphrased thus.

'All those who hunt for acceptance with God on the grounds of doing what the law commands are under the curse of God. That is clear from Scripture which says, "Everyone who fails to stand fast by everything written in the lawbook, and to do it, is under the curse of God." It is perfectly clear that no-one obtains right standing with God by law, for Scripture says, "The one who obtains right standing through faith will win life".'

10. Only a loose paraphrase such as the above can hope to bring out the meaning. Paul is deliberately contrasting *hoi ek pisteōs*, 'the men of faith' (RSV) with *hosoi ex ergōn nomou*, 'those who rely on obedience to the law' (NEB). In general terms, of course, the first correspond to the Christian and the second to the Jews. But for Paul the categories are more inclusive still, for they correspond to the only two ways in which it is possible to approach God. Either we approach Him completely without merit, on the ground of His grace alone, or we approach Him on the grounds of our own merits. In this sense Abraham 'pioneers' the first group while the Judaizers, in spite of their assertion that they believe in Jesus, support the second.

But what is *hupo kataran*, 'under curse'? There are times in the New Testament when Paul almost seems to give *orgē* (wrath) and *katara* (curse) independent existence. Indeed, in Romans we could enlarge this by adding sin, death, law, and other 'powers'. But this is not so much a theological concept of hostile powers warring against God, or of abstract forces that, once unleashed by God, must find fulfilment like Nemesis in a Greek tragedy. This is purely a Jewish form of expression; and in many cases the reason for the apparent 'abstraction' can be found in some passage from the Old Testament. In the case of *katara* there is a long history, from Genesis iii. 14–19 (where first the serpent is cursed and then the earth—the latter indirectly because of man) to Malachi ii. 2.[1] An examination of Genesis iii. 14–19, for instance (or the similar passage in Genesis iv. 11, 12), will show how closely 'the curse' is related to the reaction of God to sin. Nothing could be further from the concept of a blind depersonalized force.

'But this is all before the giving of the law', the Jew might well say. So Paul comes at once to the period after the giving of the Torah. He quotes Deuteronomy xxvii. 26 to show that failure to keep and do the law brings this same 'curse'. Now it is quite true that the Hebrew Bible does not have the word 'all' in this verse; it simply says 'Cursed be he who does not confirm the words of this law by doing them', to which all the people set their 'Amen', thus accepting the justice of the judgment. But the 'all' comes in the next verse, 'being careful to do *all* his commandments' (both translations RSV). After his fashion, therefore, Paul is probably fusing two quotations into one. Now since it was manifestly impossible to keep all the commandments of the law, that meant that, willy-nilly, all 'law-men' came under this curse. The Rabbis knew this; Paul himself knew it from his own experience. But there seemed no way out except by some clinging to the 'merits of the Fathers', and to those of Abraham in particular. That was why the Jews clung so insistently to the reassuring thought of physical descent from Abraham, and the bearing in their body of the mark that assured them of God's covenant with him. The average Jew believed whole-heartedly that no son of Abraham who was circumcised would go to Gehenna. And we may not smile when we remember how superstitiously some men can look on 'membership' of a church, or even the physical reception of water-baptism.

11. But now Paul wants to prove that it is utterly impossible for anyone to be 'put in the right' with God by 'keeping the

---

[1] In every case, *katara* is seen as distinct from *anathema*, although both are ultimately the objects of divine wrath.

law'. To Paul, the fact that no man can win to 'life' through the law (or even through 'law' as a general principle in other religions outside Judaism) is perfectly clear, apart altogether from the views of the Rabbis and his own religious experience. Scripture would not have described this other way of obtaining that which is true 'life', if there had already been a way through the law. He expresses this in compressed form here, but elsewhere he shows that this is part of his concept of Scripture. The Scripture that Paul uses is Habakkuk ii. 4, and AV renders the quotation *The just shall live by faith.* Presumably this was influenced by the same version's translation of the Old Testament original, 'The just shall live by his faith' (RSV prefers 'The righteous shall live by his faith' with 'faithfulness' suggested as an alternative in the margin).

Now this is a key verse for Paul's doctrine of 'justification by faith'. Romans i. 17 is another place where he uses it with great effect, and in Hebrews x. 38 the unknown author employs it again. Whatever our interpretation of the words in the Hebrews context (where the meaning seems closer to the original thought), the question is often asked nowadays: Is Paul fair to the verse in Habakkuk, or is he 'reading-in' a different meaning? Such a question can be answered only in the light of Paul's whole attitude to, and use of, the Old Testament.[1] No-one doubts what Paul's experience was; few would doubt that this was his interpretation of the verse. Some would say that, in view of his subsequent quotation of it, this verse was probably the key which unlocked this new spiritual truth to him. But is it a correct exegesis?

The brief answer to this question is that Paul does not prove his doctrine of 'justification by faith' from this verse; he only illustrates it. He proves it from God's ways of dealing with Abraham. This verse is nothing more than a handy peg upon which to hang a spiritual truth abundantly clear elsewhere in Scripture. Secondly, it is by no means clear that Paul is doing violence to the verse in Habakkuk, especially if we translate his quotation 'he shall gain life who is justified through faith'

[1] See E. E. Ellis, *Paul's Use of the Old Testament*, 1957, as well as the more general books by Davies, Daube, Schoeps and Munck (see pp. 9 f.).

(so NEB), or 'the faith-righteous shall live'. RSV renders it 'he who through faith is righteous shall live'. Even in the Old Testament, the line between 'trusty' and 'trusting' is a slender one, and we have already seen the ambiguity in the meaning of the New Testament word *pistoi*, 'faithful'.

From now on the argument moves rapidly and easily. We may paraphrase verses 12–14 as follows:

'Now the law is certainly not "through faith" (i.e. it has nothing to do with the notion of receiving "right standing" with God as a gracious gift, as a result of trust in Him); for Scripture says "He who performs these things will obtain life as a result of them". Christ bought us out from the sphere of the curse of the law by becoming accursed for us. The proof that He became "accursed" is seen in the Scripture, "Every man hanged upon a gallows is under a curse" (and Christ was hanged upon such a gibbet). The positive purpose of all this was so that "the blessing", mentioned in the Abraham story as applying to the non-Jewish peoples, should come to them through Jesus Christ so that, through our trust in Him, we might receive the promised gift of the Spirit.'

12. Again, by inserting the missing steps in the argument, as here, we can see more clearly the flow of Paul's thought. When he says that *the law is not of faith*, he is not referring to the law itself, but the law seen as a supposed means of earning God's favour by 'merit'. Later in this Epistle Paul will make perfectly clear that he has no opposition to the law as such. It is important to remember this, for it is an aspect of the Pauline theology which the Judaizers did not appreciate and which a casual reading of Paul's words might equally not make plain. Of course, the law as such lays down the necessity of observing the law in many places. Paul quotes Leviticus xviii. 5, 'You shall therefore keep my statutes and my ordinances, by doing which a man shall live' (RSV). Every Jew would agree that the law was a matter of 'doing'. That was axiomatic, there was no need for Paul to prove it, although he does quote this verse. Every system of 'natural religion' depends on 'doing'; and, as far as this aspect is concerned, Mosaic Judaism had become a thoroughly 'natural' system, whatever the original aim and object.

13. The word *exēgorasen*, 'bought back' (for which see Arndt-Gingrich and Deissmann, as there quoted), opens up with its ransom-metaphor a whole new area of understanding of the atonement. This is used to great effect elsewhere in the New Testament (notably 1 Pet. i. 18, 19) and by Paul himself in contexts such as that of Acts xx. 28. But since in this instance Paul is not stressing the manner of redemption, we may pass it by with this brief notice. It has a rich Old Testament history (see Is. xliii. 3, etc.). When Paul says that Christ 'bought us out' (as a man might 'buy himself out' of the Forces nowadays) from the curse brought by failure to keep the law, he uses the bold phrase *being made a curse for us*. This may be a simple use of the noun for the adjective, as taken above in the paraphrase; or NEB may be right in translating as 'by becoming for our sake an accursed thing', in which case one noun would be used for another. Perhaps the use of *hamartia*, 'sin', in 2 Corinthians v. 21 (where Christ is described as 'becoming sin' for us) is a parallel. Certainly it is equally bold, although most modern commentators understand it rather in the sense of 'sin-offering' in this context. It is at least interesting to refer back to i. 8, where Paul says that any who preach other than the true gospel are 'cursed'. It is true that the word used there is *anathema*, not *katara* as here,[1] but the two words come very close over one area of meaning as mentioned above. That which the Judaizers deserve to be, Christ willingly accepted as the place for Himself. Verse 13 echoes verse 10 with *kataratos*.

When Paul quotes Deuteronomy xxi. 23, 'a hanged man is accursed by God', he does not mean that a man is cursed by God because he is hanged, but that death by hanging was the outward sign in Israel of a man who was thus cursed. He was, in fact, hanged because he had broken the law, and this brought both curse and punishment. Thus to Paul, or any Jew, there was a peculiar appropriateness in the manner of the

---

[1] For both words see Arndt-Gingrich.

death that Christ endured. It was not only a death of shame to Jew and Gentile alike (the death of a slave, a servant), but it also symbolized the fact that the One who hung there was willingly enduring 'the curse' for us. It is true that the Roman punishment of crucifixion differed in many respects from the Jewish custom of exposing the dead bodies of criminals on stakes; but it was sufficiently close to point the moral. Christ was not 'cursed' just because the manner of His death was the cross. Nevertheless, this to Paul was yet another of those correspondences of Scripture which are too numerous to be accidental. To him, this was 'fulfilment', the giving of a deeper, richer meaning at another level.

14. Paul now shows the positive purpose of God in all this. It is the way He has chosen of fulfilling the 'promise' made to Abraham dealing with 'the Gentiles'. The words *ethnē* and *eulogia* could well be put in inverted commas (the 'Gentiles' and 'promise') for both are a deliberate reminiscence of iii. 8. Thus, to Paul, the promise to Abraham is only understandable, only finds fulfilment, in terms of Jesus Christ and His work. For a moment Paul now groups himself with the Gentiles in order to show more vividly the content of this promise (unless the use of *we* is an admission that Jew and Gentile stand together here). It is nothing less than the gift of the Spirit, the distinguishing mark of the child of God.

d. Does law annul promise? (iii. 15–18)

But surely, someone might argue, even if this were so, the law would have annulled any earlier such 'arrangements' with Abraham. Here is Paul, the ecclesiastical lawyer, at his best. He swoops like a hawk at the fancied or real opponent.

'Fellow-Christians, here is an ordinary human illustration. Even if it is only a man's last will and testament that has been ratified, no one else can set it aside or add a codicil (last phrase direct from NEB). The promises were made to Abraham "and his posterity". Scripture does not say "and to his posterities", as though referring to more than one, but, as though referring to one person only, "and to your posterity". This refers to

Christ. But my real point is this: once a will and testament has been already ratified by God, no law of four hundred and thirty years later can annul it and make void the promise it contained. I say this because, if the inheritance of salvation comes through the law, then it has ceased to be in fulfilment of a promise. But God gave it, once and for all, as a gracious gift to Abraham, by promise.' The suppressed apodosis is: 'Therefore the law could not possibly change the conditions of salvation, from undeserving reception of a promise to merited reception of desert or "wages".'

15. Paul now offers 'a human example' (RSV). In his writings he frequently appeals to aspects of law familiar to the layman in order to illustrate, if not prove, a spiritual point. Another good example is his use of the marriage laws in Romans vii. 1–3 to illustrate the possibility of a new union with Christ for those who have previously been 'wedded' to the law. His action corresponds to the Lord's practice of appealing to the knowledge and instincts of ordinary men against the theological prejudice of the theologians. Luke xiii. 15 and xiv. 5 are two examples, both drawn from the daily life of the Galilaean peasant. When Paul has proved his point at the human level, then he will apply it to the spiritual problem with the argument 'How much more. . . ?' Luke xi. 13 shows the Lord using the same process of argument.

In English, part of the play on words is lost because 'covenant' and 'will' (of a dying man) are two different words. But the Gk. *diathēkē* can be used with both senses in the New Testament (see Arndt-Gingrich). Something of this ambiguity can be kept by consistently translating as 'last will and testament', if we continually remember the 'Old Testament' and 'New Testament'. This ambiguity exists only in biblical Greek, and has a long history in the LXX. For the ordinary Gentile reader, *diathēkē* meant 'will' and nothing more, although in Classical times it had also had the sense of 'contract' (Arndt-Gingrich). *Sunthēkē*, the more common early word for 'covenant', does not occur in the New Testament. Of course, for the Gentile convert, certain difficulties occurred when God was said to make a *diathēkē*. Such could be valid only after the death of the testator, and God could not be said to die. But Hebrews ix. 15–21 shows the way in which early Christian apologetic met this difficulty triumphantly.

If we follow the argument in the Hebrews passage as normative (which it doubtless is) then, to Paul, the Will and Testament of God would have been 'ratified' to Abraham by the blood shed at the covenant sacrifice. A death has taken place: henceforward, not even a codicil can be added to the will. It certainly cannot be set aside at law—least of all, by the Torah given to Moses centuries later. In verse 17 Paul plays on the two words *prokekurōmenēn*, 'ratified already', and *akuroi*, 'rule out of court', in a way hard to reproduce in English. Both are linked closely with *kekurōmenēn*, 'ratified, executed' used here in verse 15, and the result is to tie Paul's argument very closely together. The use of *epidiatassetai*, translated in NEB 'add a codicil', is interesting. Presumably, Paul refers to those places in the Old Testament where it says, in anthropomorphic language, that 'God repented' of some proposed course of action. 1 Samuel xv. 10, 11 (in the light of 1 Samuel xiii. 13, 14) is a good example, where Saul is by-passed in favour of David. But nothing of this sort ever took place in the case of Abraham. Here Jewish and Christian theology were at one, however strongly the Jews might feel about the Torah.

16. This verse is a highly compressed 'inset' which somewhat complicates the argument, but may be temporarily omitted without harm. Paul is simply concerned to make two points, elsewhere elaborated. First, such a 'will' (necessarily involving promise for the future, as all wills must do) was in fact made, with Abraham as a beneficiary. Secondly, his 'offspring' was named as a further beneficiary—and this 'offspring', at the deepest level, was Jesus Christ. The second point is not really necessary here, but is a help to understanding the 'suppressed members' of Paul's argument. Once again, Paul knows as well as any other scholar that *sperma*, 'seed', can have a collective sense even in the singular. There would have been no need to use the plural to cover the meaning 'descendants'. He is saying, in typically Jewish fashion, that there is an appropriateness in the use of the singular here in that the true fulfilment is only in connection with Christ. Here all must agree: and some at least will agree with Paul that such 'appropriateness' is not without the controlling guidance of the Holy Spirit.[1] Later, Paul himself will use *sperma* in the collective sense.

17. The *four hundred and thirty years* between Abraham and Torah comes from Exodus xii. 40 (MT) and is actually the figure given there for the sojourn in Egypt. Versions vary greatly in the duration of the stay, and numbers are notoriously difficult to transmit in manuscripts. But the round figure has no interest in itself, except to show the comparative lateness of the Torah: and whether it be by one century or four, there is no gainsaying this point.

18. The word *klēronomia*, translated in the paraphrase as 'inheritance of salvation' (see Arndt-Gingrich for the *nuance*), means the actual 'enjoyment' of the benefits already promised under the will. Paul will return to this concept in iv. 1, where the Christian is *klēronomos*, 'heir'. In Scripture, the *klēronomia* is inseparable from the gift of the Spirit, the *arrabōn*, 'pledge', of our inheritance (Eph. i. 14). Similarly, when Paul speaks of *epangelia*, *promise*, here, he is undoubtedly thinking in the first place of God's great promise to Abraham. But it is hard to avoid the conclusion that he is also thinking, in a specifically New Testament sense, of the gift of the Spirit, as in verse 14. Similarly, when he uses *kecharistai*, 'given freely', to describe God's attitude to Abraham, he is thinking of the deeper connotation of *charis* to the Christian. For the believer, God's 'grace' is Christ. Paul's use of the perfect tense in this verb is probably deliberate. He wants to stress the 'once-for-allness' of God's grace; no later system of law can alter such a gift to man.

---

[1] Daube (p. 438) has an excellent discussion of this 'generic singular', showing the rabbinic parallels for such arguments.

e. What is the purpose of the law? (iii. 19–29)

Paul has now proved his point, certainly to his own satisfaction; perhaps even the Galatian converts are convinced. But he may have proved too much. It looks as if there is no place left for the law at all. Doubtless, this would not have troubled the Galatians, though it would ultimately have made their judgment of the Jerusalem church quite unfair. But the Judaizers would have pounced on it at once. Not only was Paul's evangel antinomian in practice—it was even antinomian in theory. This was the charge that was already circulating at Jerusalem, and to which James refers in Acts xxi. 21. Further, Paul's own consistency demanded that he give the law its rightful place in God's historical plan. He was never more truly a Jew than when he was a Christian. In chapters v and vi, he will show that 'justification by faith' cannot lead to antinomianism; it is instead the door to holy living. Elsewhere, he will show that the law has a present value in the life of the Christian; but there is no need to do this at the moment in Galatia where its place is already being over-stressed. All he needs to do, in order to clear himself of false charges and also to show the consistency of God, is to demonstrate the place of the Torah in God's plan of salvation for man.

'Why then the Law? It was added as a supplement because of sins—valid until the "posterity" arrived to whom the promise had been made in the will. Yes, it was negotiated through angels; yes, it was done through a middleman; but the very presence of a middleman implies more than one party, and our creed is that "God is one". Does that mean that the law is directly opposed to the promises? An impossible thought. If the kind of law had been given which could give "life", then it would have been true that right standing with God came from law. But the Scripture (sc. 'of the Torah') groups everything under the general heading of "sin", so that the promise attendant on faith in Jesus Christ might be given to those who believe.'

19. The little phrase *tōn parabaseōn charin* is not easy to interpret, although the meaning *because of transgressions* or 'sins' is plain. Paul may mean 'to restrain fallen human nature'. In that sense the law would have a temporary moral value, but it would be concessive. Until Christ had come, men had neither the moral incentive nor the moral pattern that alone would make Christian freedom something different from libertinism. NEB, however, takes a stronger approach with 'to make wrongdoing a legal offence'. This may well be correct. It would link with Paul's words in verse 22, and his own moral experience depicted in Romans vii. Indeed, there are times when Paul boldly says that the function of the law was not to make us holy but to give us an awakened sense of sin. Put in this way, the function of the 'moral sense' is to teach us our own moral bankruptcy, and the function of intellect is to teach us the intellectual bankruptcy of fallen mankind. But although Paul is certainly capable of adopting as strong a position there is no need to postulate it here.

The Jewish belief in the angelic mediation of the law is shown in Stephen's speech (see Acts vii. 53). Here Paul, like Stephen, is being strictly orthodox. Like the author of the Epistle to the Hebrews he will admit any Jewish claim before showing how each such claim is transcended in Christ. Perhaps this Jewish stress on angels is responsible for the care with which the Gospel writers record all angelic visitations in connection with the birth of Jesus, in whom God was to reveal Himself directly. Was the Torah revealed through angels? Then how much more was Jesus Christ!

20. Having admitted the mediatorial work of Moses, Paul seems to be claiming that this is a weakness, rather than a strength, of the law. His thought seems to be that, in His promise, God has dealt directly with mankind. It is true that there is, in Christian thought, 'one Mediator' (1 Tim. ii. 5). But Christ is God as well as man and thus, in Christ, God is still dealing directly with man. In the *Theos heis estin, God is one*, Paul seems to be appealing to Israel's age-old creed; no Jew would dare to dispute that for a moment.

21. He has proved that the law cannot annul the promise

of God. But is it some sort of ineffectual opposition to promise? No. Paul's brief dismissal of the idea with the words *mē genoito*, 'may it never be so', shows that such a thought comes near blasphemy, for it would imply inner conflict within the mind of God. Promise is from God; law is equally from God. It only remains to relate them in one coherent system. Clearly the purpose of the law was not to give that eschatological 'life' which is one of the many words for 'salvation'. If the Torah had been able to do that, then there might indeed have been some opposition between law and promise. But as it is, the function of the Torah was to bring to men that clearer knowledge of the character and demands of God which would, in its turn, bring a deeper consciousness of sin. Revelation is not favouritism; it is a heavy burden of responsibility. We have no excuse, for we are the servants who knew what the will of our Master was and yet disobeyed (Lk. xii. 47). Paul does not say that Gentiles knew nothing of God's law (see Rom. i. 19, 20), but he does claim that the Jew has a far deeper insight into God's will (Rom. ii. 17, 18), and that this only condemns him the more.

22. So it is that the law *sunekleisen*, 'grouped' (or perhaps 'imprisoned'), everything within the frontiers of acknowledged sin. We are all, Jew or Gentile, on the same footing. When Paul says *hē graphē* here, he is almost certainly thinking of the Scriptures of the Law, and the phrase has been thus translated in the paraphrase. Romans iii. 9–20 will prove the same truth from those parts of the Old Testament known as the Prophets and Writings; but Paul has a peculiar concern with the third section, the Law, at the moment.

In recent years there has been much study of the phrase *ta panta*, 'everything', especially in connection with Paul's concept of 'cosmic redemption', as in Ephesians i. 22. Romans viii. 22 also has some bearing. But here Paul's meaning is probably only 'all men', referring to sin's universality, rather than to its cosmic aspect.

Were Paul to stop with the negative aspect of his doctrine of the place and purpose of the law we should indeed be in a terrible plight. But to him the purpose of classifying us all as 'sinners' (and making us accept the justice of this classification) is solely so that we may be eligible for salvation. Righteous men have no claim on Christ; it was to save sinners that He came (Mt. ix. 12, 13). Seen from this angle, the operation of the law is all of grace; and this is what Paul has already insisted in the second half of verse 22. He will now expand his meaning in verses 23–26.

'Before Christian faith had entered the scene, we were held under arrest by law, kept in gaol, awaiting the divine revelation of that faith that was to come. Seen in this light, the law was our "escort" to lead us to Christ so that we might be justified by trust. But once faith has come we are no longer under the authority of our "escort"; for we are all God's sons, through trust in Christ Jesus.'

This passage is full of semi-personifications. *ho nomos* can easily be translated as 'the Law', with special reference to the Law of Moses, and *nomos* as 'law', seen as a general principle. But the use of the article with *pistis*, 'faith', is more ambiguous. Does he mean 'Faith' as a principle, or 'the Christian faith' with special reference to that attitude of conscious dependence upon God which is possible only to those who have heard and accepted the 'good news' as it is in Christ? Probably in Paul's mind there would be no contradiction, and thus we may translate it as 'the Faith', in the sense in which the word is used in later church history. 1 Timothy iv. 1 may be another early instance of this usage.

23. *ephrouroumetha* is translated by NEB as 'we were . . . in the custody of law'. In itself it has the idea of 'guarding' as much as that of 'confining'; perhaps 'in protective custody' would give the sense better. The word *sunkleiomenoi* (NEB, 'we were close prisoners') makes plain that some form of restrictive confinement is intended. It is a deliberate echo of *sunekleisen* in verse 22. But, even taking all this together, the law is no grim captor—particularly in view of the fact that we are only being held in custody pending the arrival of a Queen's pardon. It is typical of Paul that he sees the need for revelation in connection with this gift of faith. The word *apokaluphthēnai, to be revealed*, expresses the same truth as i. 12. Without a prior act of God, we cannot even believe in Him. That is why not even faith itself is meritorious in Paul's eyes (Eph. ii. 8).

24. Paul himself apparently feels it necessary to correct the possible idea that the law is a surly gaoler, and so, by a quick shift of metaphor, he transforms law into a *paidagōgos*, an escort for children. Those who can remember the stern, old-fashioned 'children's nanny' or the even more old-fashioned governess will have a fair idea of the position and duties of the trusty, elderly slave who conducted his young master to and from school.[1] The only ambiguity lies in the two words *eis Christon, unto Christ*. The possible translations are well expressed in NEB text, 'until Christ should come' and NEB mg., 'to conduct us to Christ'. In view of the function of the 'tutor' in the ancient world, perhaps the second is preferable. The law too, Paul is saying, was designed to teach us the great truth that only through faith in Christ could we be justified, although its part in this process was negative, not positive. So far from the law being contradictory to 'the promise', or even irrelevant, Paul has shown that the law is indispensable.

25. But, like the child's escort, it had its definite place in history. Once the faith-principle is operative, there is no room for that of law. The two cannot co-exist at the same time (as the Judaizers think) since the function of law is essentially preparatory. To return to Paul's human analogy; once the boy has grown up, he is no longer under the control of the 'nanny'. Faith in Christ has given him full sonship of God, and the restraints of the past are gone. It is possible that Paul may have been thinking of the respect traditionally due to the 'tutor', even after the child has attained his majority. Some such thought is clearly present in 1 Corinthians iv. 15, but it is not actually expressed here. Such respect the Christian would always have for the law, both because of its place in the history of salvation and because of the abiding witness that it gives to the character of God.

[1] For a study of the word see Arndt-Gingrich with the literature there quoted.

26. It is uncertain whether we should translate 'sons of God through faith in Christ Jesus' or 'faith-children of God in the corporate whole that is the Body of Christ'. NEB seems to favour this latter, with 'sons of God in union with Christ Jesus'. The grammar would favour the first, but the subsequent train of thought would favour the second.

Strictly, this is more a matter of theological interpretation than linguistics; it hinges on the meaning of the great Pauline phrase *en Christō*, 'in Christ', for which see Arndt-Gingrich, with relevant literature quoted there. Briefly, this is the Pauline (and Johannine) expression to denote the closeness of the relation of the individual to Christ. It implies a closeness of communion which is neither absorption nor complete identification (see note on ii. 20); for, while personality may be changed, it is not obliterated. It is the collective whole of all Christians that is termed 'the Body of Christ', not the individual. In this whole each 'limb' has a distinctive part to play (Rom. xii. 4 ff. and 1 Cor. xii. 20). There is a closely related metaphor by which the body of the individual Christian may be described as a 'temple of the Holy Spirit' and the collective whole may equally be so described (1 Cor. vi. 19 and 1 Cor. iii. 16 respectively; but many other examples could be given). John describes this type of continual and total dependence as 'abiding' in Christ (see Jn. xv).

Paul now develops this thought of our sonship of God, through faith in Christ.

'For all those of you who have been baptized into Jesus Christ have clothed yourselves with Christ. In Him, there is no such distinction as Jew and non-Jew, slave and freeman, male and female. You are all an entity in Christ Jesus. But if you are joined to Christ (lit. 'Christ's'), then you are collectively the "posterity of Abraham" already mentioned; you are the beneficiaries of the promise in the will.'

27. It is presumably the relationship summed up in the words 'in Christ' (see note on verse 26) to which Paul refers in the phrase *baptized into Christ*. Baptism, with its picture of death and new life and the passing of the 'waters of judgment' over the head of the sinner, symbolizes and seals the ending of an old relationship and the beginning of a new. Ideally, it should correspond to the dawn of new life in the heart of the convert. But even in the pages of the New Testament we find the Spirit coming before baptism, during baptism, after baptism—and apparently not coming at all sometimes (see the accounts of Ananias and Simon Magus—Acts v. 1–11, viii. 9–24). Not only does baptism fitly express the establishment of a new personal relationship with Christ; it is also the outward means by which we enter that collective whole which is the Church, the body of Christ. So closely does Paul associate the outward sign with the inward grace that there are times when he uses of the outward rite expressions which are, theologically speaking, more properly applied to the spiritual change. But this is a continual phenomenon in the Bible and does not necessarily mean that he identified the two. Here Paul juxtaposes two verbs, the one strictly descriptive of a physical experience, the other of a spiritual, without any consciousness of incongruity. We who were baptized *have put on Christ*, like a garment (so NEB). For the word *enedusasthe*, see Arndt-Gingrich. The figure probably comes from the Old Testament where, for instance, the Spirit 'clothes Himself' with Gideon, 'puts on' Gideon, as it were (Jdg. vi. 34). The word has a rich metaphorical use both in and outside the New Testament, especially in connection with moral qualities. Bold though this figure is, it can be paralleled almost exactly in pagan literature in the sense of 'assume the role of', although the Christian usage means far more than this. The use of 'stripping' and 'putting on' may derive, in Christian circles, from the undressing before baptism, and the subsequent dressing (no doubt from earliest days wherever possible) in clean white clothing. But it is peculiarly appropriate as describing a situation where certain habits and qualities have to be laid aside for ever and a new set assumed.

28. In the New Testament *eni* stands for *enesti*; but it seems always to be used in the negative sense. In the collective whole which is 'the body of Christ' there is no longer any place for the traditional distinctions that divide mankind—cultural, linguistic, religious (for *Greek*, opposed to *Jew*, conveys all of these) or sexual. Some have seen here a thrust at the Judaizers. The Jewish male gave regular thanks to God that he was not born a Gentile or a woman, while the woman dolefully thanked God that she was made as she was. Paul would then be pointing out that, in Christ, the 'party walls' that were accepted, and even extolled, in Judaism had been broken down (Eph. ii. 14). But it may simply be that these were types of division familiar to his hearers, and that he uses them to symbolize all such human divisions.

Paul bases his strong position (the abolition of such distinctions) on the grounds that all are now *heis*, 'one man' or 'an entity', in Christ. (NEB translates 'one person', thus making the meaning doubly sure.) Here again is the concept of the collective whole. It is a short step from this to the use of the 'body-concept' which sees the totality of believers as the body of Christ.

29. That the use of the masculine ('one person') rather than the neuter ('one thing') is no accident is shown by the next verse. Literally it says 'if you are Christ's' (so RSV); but the meaning is stronger than this. NEB translates 'if you thus belong to Christ'. But we might almost paraphrase 'if you are part of Christ's body'. Paul is going to apply to the collective whole of the Christian Church that which he has previously predicated of Christ in person—the inheritance of the Abrahamic promise. Those who thus are Christ's are (collectively) the 'offspring' (singular again) mentioned in the famous passage in Genesis, and thus the 'heirs' (plural, for we severally enjoy the benefits) in fulfilment of God's promise. This in itself will show that Paul's insistence on the use of the singular in iii. 16 is more an exegetic device than anything else. Once we see that the primary reference is to Christ, he is prepared to allow that there is a secondary reference to all Christians, as being 'in Him'.

f. The difference between son and infant (iv. 1–11)

There are certain pictures which captured Paul's imagination and which he therefore tended to use again and again. Human growth was one of these. Here he uses the image with reference to mental and intellectual development rather than to physical. This again is a favourite aspect with him (cf. 1 Cor. xiii. 11). If we are to look for a link with the argument of chapter iii, it is probably to be found in the thought of the child's being led to and from school by the *paidagōgos* while still in his minority.

'What I am saying is this: as long as the heir is a young child, he is no better than a slave, even though he is the owner of all; he is under guardians and administrators until the time that his father has fixed (i.e. in his last will and testament). So too we, when we were "young children", were kept in slavery to the ABC of the universe. But when the time had fully passed, God sent out His own Son, woman-born, born under the conditions of law, so that He might "buy out" those under the conditions of law, in order that ours might be the privilege of adoption. Because you are sons, God has sent His Son's spirit into your hearts. It is that Spirit who cries within us "My father". So that makes you, not slave, but son; and, as surely as you are a son, you are an heir by God's gift.'[1]

1. *Nēpios*, 'young child', should really mean 'babe', and there are places where Paul thus uses it. For example, in 1 Corinthians iii. 1, the *nēpios* is one who is still on 'milk', unable to face the 'solid food' of Christian doctrine. Here, however, NEB may be correct in translating simply 'a minor'; for the main point is that the child is not yet old enough to fulfil the terms of his father's will. But if *stoicheia*, *elements*, in verse 3 does mean 'ABC', as some have held, then perhaps Paul is thinking of a child of kindergarten age. Such a child is 'no better off than a slave' (NEB): *diapherei*, *differeth*, usually has this sense of 'surpassing'.

2. Paul does not introduce the *paidagōgos* here, for he is not so much thinking of the child's education as the administration of the estate which, though his by right, is not yet his to manage. Otherwise, the *epitropous* and *oikonomous*, *tutors* and *governors* (RSV, NEB, 'guardians and trustees') answer fairly

---

[1] It will be convenient to break the paraphrase here, at verse 7; the next three verses will further elaborate the meaning of one term in this passage.

closely to the 'tutor' in iii. 25 above. It is probably fanciful to see any theological distinction. The law was our *paidagōgos*, but that does not necessarily mean that something other than the Torah was our *epitropos* or *oikonomos*. Both of these could easily stand for the law as well in its other aspects. Again, much hinges on the meaning of *stoicheia tou kosmou*, 'elemental things of the universe', in the next verse, and whether it applies to the Jewish law or no. It is conceivable that Paul does make a slight distinction in his mind, and thinks of the 'guardians' and 'administrators' as those who taught, rather than the law which was taught. In that case, the two words could well stand for the Judaizers in their proselytizing activity in Galatia. Paul would then be saying: in the past you may well have been under such men—but not now.

For *prothesmia*, see Arndt-Gingrich and the literature there quoted. The best translation seems to be *time appointed*, 'date set' (RSV), referring to the father's legal right to fix the day when his son would 'come of age', for the purpose of inheriting his father's property. For Paul, this is connected with the concept *plērōma tou chronou*, *the fulness of the time*, found here in verse 4. To Paul, this is when, in the plan of God, all mankind attains its majority in the coming of Christ. The use of the word *plērōma* may not be unconnected with the Jewish teaching being given in Galatia at the time. The later Jewish gnostics made great play with the word in their theological systems, and Paul counters with his Christological teaching in Ephesians and Colossians. But it is not necessary to see this undercurrent in the present passage where his thoughts are still on the legal illustration before him.

3. Much will therefore depend on the meaning of *stoicheia tou kosmou*, *the elements of the world* (RSV, NEB, 'universe'). In earlier Greek *stoicheia* can certainly mean 'elementary principles', or even 'alphabet' (and so it has been translated in the running paraphrase above). This, or something very similar, must be the meaning in Hebrews v. 12, and may well be the meaning both in the present passage and in Colossians ii. 8 and 20. In that case, Paul will be referring to the elementary stages of religious experience (whether Jewish or Gentile) through which they have gone in the past, but which are now out-dated by Christ. There have been great names in support of this, as can be seen from the foot of the relevant article in Arndt-Gingrich. The advantage is that this applies equally to Jew and Gentile; for if the Galatians had been Gentile pagans before they were converted, they could scarcely have been said to have been in slavery to the Jewish law, no matter from what angle it was considered. NEB mg. takes this view, cautiously, translating 'elementary ideas belonging to this world'.

Most modern commentators, however, prefer to translate either as 'elemental spirits' of this world (so RSV, NEB) or possibly 'the signs of the zodiac', which often represented them in popular belief. Earth, air, fire, water ('the elements') and the stars were often linked in men's minds with vague spiritual forces, as in astrology even today. In view of verse 10, with its reference to careful observation of a 'calendar', some have felt that such an interpretation suited the strange syncretistic Judaism that we know to have existed at the time, especially in Asia Minor. This was the soil from which later Jewish Gnosticism (as distinct from purely pagan Gnosticism) was to grow. On the other hand, if the Judaizers were strictly orthodox Jews (as Acts seems to suggest), they would abhor this as much as Paul did. Every Jew believed fervently that the Exile had been due to the 'star-worship' of Manasseh and others like him (cf. Je. xliv). If the Galatians had been pagans before conversion, then such astrological speculation would have formed part of their religious system, whatever god's name they might actually use in worship.

In verse 9, Paul calls the 'elements' *asthenē kai ptōcha*, 'weak and poor'. This does not really help us to fix the meaning more precisely; it merely gives Paul's opinion as to their comparative worthlessness. Colossians ii. 8 and 20 seem to represent a developed use of the word which may not, therefore, have exactly the same meaning. In verse 8, it is associated closely with 'philosophy' and 'tradition'—which at once suggests some esoteric system—and, significantly, with *plērōma* close by. In both verse 8 and verse 20 these *stoicheia* are contrasted sharply with Christ, as in the Galatians passage.[1]

4. In the statement that God *exapesteilen, sent forth* ('sent on a mission') *his Son*, it is tempting to see an allusion to the title *apostolos*, 'apostle', over which there had apparently been controversy between the Jerusalem church and Paul. It is noteworthy that, after the admission of i. 17 (where Paul includes himself in the number), he does not in this letter use the title 'apostle' of the leaders at Jerusalem. (Cf. 2 Corinthians xi. 5, where he calls them 'super-apostles', no doubt with his tongue in his cheek.) The application of the term to Christ would not, of course, be isolated: Hebrews iii. 1 applies the noun to Him directly as God's unique 'messenger' or 'delegate'.[2]

When Christ is described as *genomenon ek gunaikos*, 'woman-born', the reference is probably to His full humanity as well as deity, rather than a direct reference to the virgin birth, though such could well be included. That Paul does not deal with this doctrine directly does not prove that he was not cognizant with it. If Luke, the author of the Gospel, was also the author of Acts and travel-companion of Paul, it is inconceivable that Paul should have been ignorant of the birth-stories of Luke i, ii. For a Jew, whether Paul or a Judaizer, the chief relevance of such a phrase would be its correspondence with Genesis iii. 15. Here at last is the promised 'seed' of the woman who will crush the serpent's head. Paul would no doubt also think of the promise of Isaiah vii. 14 concerning the birth of Immanuel.

Not only was Christ born as man, He was born 'under conditions of law'. This is probably a reference to His birth in the Jewish race, although, as *nomos* has no article, it could be argued that this is simply a reference to His status as man. To Paul, all men are under *nomos* of some kind; only Jews, however, are under *ho nomos*, the law of Moses. Elsewhere the New Testament develops the twin concepts that Christ came to

[1] In addition to the standard Bible Dictionaries and Wordbooks, the thoughtful excursus in Burton may be consulted with profit.
[2] See the Appendix in Burton.

fulfil the law, and that Christ perfectly kept the law. Here Paul mentions only His 'status', as it were. His real reason for mentioning it at all is that it introduces the next clause.

5. Christ was born under law-conditions so that He might ransom those who were themselves under such conditions. In iii. 13 it was from the 'curse of the law' that we were redeemed; here the figure is bolder. We are redeemed from the law itself, seen as a system of attempted self-justification. Whether *apolabōmen* has anything of the sense 'get back' or not is uncertain; it may simply be 'attain' (NEB) with no thought of the privileges lost by the fall. *Huiothesian* is a fully legal term, *adoption*, though in the New Testament it is only used in a religious sense. The idea, although not the word, is Old Testament, referring to the status given to Israel by God and the new relationship into which she had been called. It is, however, not such an abstract word as 'adoption' in English; perhaps, therefore, the NEB translation 'the status of sons' is preferable. The use of the definite article with the noun, *tēn huiothesian* ('the adoption'), may just be to mark it as an abstract noun. On the other hand, it may mean 'the famous Adoption, of which Scripture speaks'.

6. Now the action quickens. It is because you are sons, says Paul, that *God hath sent forth the Spirit of his Son into your hearts*. If it were possible to isolate stages in what is one spiritual process, we should say that this was necessary to make adoptive sons true-born. For it is by the presence of the Spirit in our hearts that we are assured of our sonship of God (Rom. viii. 16) and enabled to pray with confidence.[1]

Exactly the same word (*exapesteilen*) is used of God's action in sending the Spirit as has already been used in verse 4 of His sending the Son. It is not strange, therefore, that the Spirit is here described as *the Spirit of his Son*. This is no confusion of two persons of the Trinity, but simply a recognition of the close link that exists in Scripture. The Spirit was the promise of the Son (Jn. xiv) as well as of the Father. It is by the Spirit

---

[1] It is interesting that in the Romans passage, too, the word *Abba* recurs, suggesting a definite thought-link.

that Christ lives in our hearts (Eph. iii. 16, 17). Indeed, so close is the link that, without the Spirit, a man does not belong to Christ (Rom. viii. 9). There is also another sense in which such a phrase is appropriate; the Spirit rested on Christ in all His fullness (Jn. iii. 34), and Christ, in the obedience of His life and death, showed, as none other ever could, the meaning of the Spirit of sonship. *Abba*, 'father', is one of the Aramaic 'fossils' in the New Testament. It was the very word used by Christ in prayer as recorded in Mark xiv. 36. As such, it seems to have passed into the prayer life of the primitive Church, even where the language used was Greek. While it was the usual informal word applied by a child to its father within the home, it is over-sentimentalizing to translate it as 'Daddy'.

7. Yet the use of this intimate word is, to Paul, the proof that we have that 'inner witness' of the Spirit within our hearts; that in itself convinces us that we are sons, not slaves.[1] The Greek *ei*, *if*, does not imply any doubt; NEB is correct in translating 'then also'. As surely as we are sons we are God's heirs by His own gift; the two concepts are inseparable to Paul. The contrast of 'slave' and 'son' is familiar from John xv. 15.

Verses 8–10 are an elaboration of the nature of the Galatian error, and interesting from that point of view. The passage represents, however, a slight excursus, and does not itself lead the argument any further.

'But in those days, when you were without knowledge of God, you were slaves to those things which by their very nature are No-Gods. But now that you do know God—or rather, now that God knows you—how is it that you are continually harking back to these powerless and limited elementary practices? Do you want to be their slaves all over again? I am referring to the way in which you keep special days, and months, and seasons, and years. I am afraid that I may have wasted all my pains on you.'

---

[1] Romans viii. 26 further discusses the function of the Spirit in connection with our prayer-life, and indeed our whole relationship with God.

8. The contrast between God and not-gods is typically Jewish; this sort of word-play was very congenial to the Hebrew language. The use of *phusei*, 'by birth', 'by nature', is interesting. Just as Paul had pointed out to Peter that they two were Jews 'naturally', so here he points out that, by the very nature of the case, these 'elements' could not be gods. Had he enlarged on this theme, it would doubtless have involved the Hebrew doctrine of creation. To Paul, the great sin of idolatry is to worship the created thing rather than the creator (Rom. i. 25); and whether it be the 'elements' or the 'heavenly bodies', all are the work of God's hand.

9. In the Bible 'to know' has a far deeper meaning than the superficial concept of intellectual knowledge alone. That is why it can be used of the relation of God and man, and of the peculiarly intimate relation of husband and wife. But it is typical of Paul's strong theological position that he is reluctant to speak of men 'knowing' God; rather, he corrects it to the passive 'having become objects of the divine recognition'. That transfers salvation altogether out of the possibly subjective and illusory into the great objective reality of the will of God.

Of course, the Judaizers do not consciously intend to 'enslave' the Galatians; nor do the Galatians consciously intend to re-enter spiritual slavery. But since this will be the inevitable consequence of their actions, Paul wishes to shock them into the realization of what, all unknowing, they are doing at the very moment.

10. It is not certain whether the 'elements' are identified with these 'times and seasons', now being observed in Galatia, or whether such customs are but an example of 'returning to the infants' class' in the religious world. The *days* could refer to the liturgical calendar of orthodox Judaism, with its 'new moons' and 'sabbatical years'. They could equally refer to the quasi-magical observances that we know to have been rife in Ephesus and, presumably, in other parts of Asia Minor (Acts xix). Heterodox Jews certainly practised these arts, as we see from Acts xix. 13. In inter-testamental days, the Jews displayed immense interest in the calendar, probably considered from this 'lucky days' aspect. Where observance of a Christian 'liturgical year' has become a similar bondage, it is interesting to speculate what Paul's views would have been on the matter. It is not necessary, however, to see any Jewish influence in these Galatian customs; in all forms of paganism there is some form of 'casting horoscopes', with consequent 'lucky' and 'unlucky' days.

11. With *eikē, in vain* 'to no purpose', Paul is returning to the thought of iii. 4. There he is asking whether the Galatians themselves may not have gone through such initial spiritual experiences to no purpose. Here the thought is rather that he may have wasted all his pains in preaching to them. It is doubtful if these verses can be used, either way, to illustrate Paul's views on Christian security after salvation. Even in iii. 4 his desire to win back the Galatians will not allow him to consider this 'loss' as a serious possibility.

The word *kekopiaka*, 'I toiled', implies hard work leading to real weariness; it is a favourite word with Paul to explain the trials of the Christian ministry. If those to whom he writes are the inhabitants of the cities of South Galatia, then we know from Acts xiii and xiv something of the 'toil' involved. This verb (which has a good sense) should be distinguished from the *kopous parechetō*, 'give me trouble', of vi. 17, which has a bad meaning.

g. A personal appeal for better relations (iv. 12–20)

Perhaps it is the thought of all that he has endured on their behalf which now turns the Epistle in a more personal direction. On the whole (and in contrast with 2 Corinthians) the whole argument, while intensely emotional, has been strangely impersonal. One suspects that, at times, Paul is either grappling with the problem or thinking of his Judaizing opponents rather than thinking of the local Christians with whom he must have had so many individual bonds. The strongest term of affection that he has so far allowed himself in the whole letter is *adelphoi*, 'Christian brothers'; and this is a very general term within the Christian community. He will use the term again here; but he will go far beyond it in reminiscence.

'I ask you to imagine yourselves in my position, fellow-Christians, just as I have imagined myself in yours. Your attitude to me was once quite correct. You know that in sickness of body I preached the good news to you before, and you neither made little of the bodily trials that I had, nor felt any revulsion. You welcomed me as God's own messenger, like Jesus Christ Himself. What has happened to the blessing that you enjoyed then? I can bear witness myself that, if you could have taken out your own eyes and given them to me, you would have done so. So now I have become your enemy by acting faithfully towards you, have I?

'These others are envious of you, and their envy has an evil aim. They want to exclude you (sc. "from blessing" or "from my love") so that you may come to envy them their position. Envy in a good cause is always good, not only when I am with you, my dear spiritual children. I have all the pains of child-labour over again for you, until Christ takes shape in you. Only I do wish that I could be with you now, and change my tone; for I really do not know what to do in your case.'[1]

This passage bristles with difficulties, although fortunately none of them are of a serious nature and none of them raise theological problems. If we knew more of the relations of Paul with these 'Galatians', doubtless much would be clear. As it is, those who favour a South Galatian destination scent references to the Acts account at every turn. True, if the letter be written to Galatians of the north, we are completely without a clue as to the meaning of the references. But we are not even sure that the account in Acts represents the full story of the evangelization of the south, so that we are little better off either way. Fortunately, the Greek is fairly straightforward, and the manuscript variation insignificant. All turns on the exact interpretation.

12. The opening clause is the first puzzle. Literally it reads 'Be like me, as I too (have become) like you'. NEB is probably right in turning it, 'Put yourselves in my place . . . for I have

---

[1] The above translation assumes that *zēloō* means 'to envy', and not 'to court the favour of'. See detailed discussion below.

put myself in yours.' That Paul does not, in point of fact, continue in this vein is no argument that he may not have started thus. On the other hand, he may simply mean, 'Be as frank and loving with me as I have always been with you.' Either way, it is clearly a personal appeal to the Galatians to resume their old friendly terms with Paul which have apparently been ruptured by the work of the Judaizers. The exact details need not detain us.

When Paul says *ye have not injured me*, is he stating a fact, or is he quoting, in indignation, a presumed remark of the Galatians? 'Never wronged me, did you?' In support of his indignation he would then contrast their past behaviour with their present. It seems undoubted that in the Corinthian correspondence Paul frequently uses this device of putting a sentence into the mouth of his opponents only to confute it. As there is no other instance in Galatians, however, this is perhaps the less likely explanation of the two.

13. Paul preached to these Galatians, whoever they were, *di' astheneian*, which may mean 'amid bodily weakness' or 'because of bodily weakness'. Much profitless argument has raged around these few words. Those who favour a South Galatian destination are apt to see a reference to the stoning recorded in Acts xiv, and perhaps some consequent physical debility. But the stoning itself was not a 'bodily weakness', and Scripture does not mention any such permanent result, though it is always possible. It seems better, therefore, to take it as a general reference. Again, on the supposition that it was a fever of malarial type, much discussion has raged on whether the southern plateau was malarial, or the coastal belt through which the missionaries had just passed. Others have argued that the fresh breezes of the northern plateau were just what was needed for a sick man. But, unfortunately, the Bible does not tell us that Paul had any such fever. In fact, the passage before us suggests that it was rather some constitutional infirmity to which Paul was constantly subject. As to its nature, we can do no more than guess. If that is so, and the reference is general, then it is probably correct to translate 'amid bodily weakness' (rather than NEB, 'it was bodily illness that originally led to my bringing you the Gospel'). We have no reference in Acts to any occasion in the Galatic region where sickness or infirmity led to a longer stay than intended, with consequent opportunities for evangelism. On the other hand, it does seem as though Paul was constantly plagued by ill-health. However, the list of Paul's hairbreadth escapes in 2 Corinthians xi warns us that the account in Acts is not complete, but a highly compressed and selective account of what is regarded as significant incident. 2 Corinthians xii. 7 seems to describe Paul's constant malady as *skolops tē sarki*, 'a stake thrust into my body', which suggests intense pain.

In the paraphrase above, *to proteron* has been translated simply as 'before': NEB text takes this view with 'originally', although the NEB mg. gives the classical meaning of the phrase with 'on the first of my two visits'. If this last translation were certain, it would have bearing both on the date and the destination of the letter. We might see, for instance, a reference to the two trips through South Galatia in the first missionary journey. If it has to be North Galatia, the date would be much later, and indeed to fit in two trips at all would give us considerable difficulty unless we fell back on the convenient hypothesis of the 'silences of Acts'. But as in Hellenistic Greek the word *proteron* has a greatly weakened meaning, probably 'formerly' is quite sufficient. The same problem, in outline, arose in connection with *palin*, 'again', in ii. 1 (although many Fathers omit the *palin* there).

14. Most scholars have taken *peirasmos*, *temptation* or 'trial', as being synonymous with Paul's 'thorn in the flesh' (2 Cor. xii. 7). But there is at least some MS evidence to suggest that it should rather be 'the trial that you endured through the condition of my body' (cf. RSV). This reading is more difficult, so it may be right. The *peirasmos* would then be the 'temptation' to despise Paul because of his physical ailment. If this ailment was not only incapacitating but also unsightly, the word would take on a deeper meaning. In that case, we should follow NEB with 'you resisted any temptation to show scorn or disgust at the state of my poor body'. This is a little free, but it links the 'temptation' satisfactorily with the *exouthenēsate*, 'scorned', and *exeptusate*, 'spat in contempt', immediately below. But, attractive though this explanation is, the object of these two verbs is clearly *ton peirasmon*, 'the trial'; therefore it is better to take the 'trial' as a direct reference to Paul's bodily complaint, whatever it was. In that case, *exouthenēsate*, though nominally applied to Paul's disease, is really applied to Paul.[1]

Since *diaptuō* can certainly mean 'reject contemptuously', it is likely that *ekptuō* is similarly used here, with no memory of the literal meaning of 'spit out'.[2] On the grounds that sight of a madman or an epileptic demanded 'prophylactic spitting' on the part of bystanders some have claimed that Paul's trouble was epilepsy. But this is not the Epistle of an epileptic (such in Jewish eyes would have been probably classed as demon possessed). In any case, such evidence is far too slender; no case can be based on it alone. A third interesting possibility is that Paul is harking back to the thought of iii. 1, the 'evil eye' (*tis ebaskanen*, 'who bewitched you?'). The protective act against suspected 'evil eye' was to spit. Does Paul mean that, although the Judaizers have 'bewitched' the Galatians, they never had reason to feel that he had done so? Or—perhaps fancifully—was there something about the 'piercing eyes' of Paul, described by tradition, that might well have made them uneasy and afraid? If Paul suffered from some ailment of the eyes, perhaps his very appearance could have suggested such magical powers to superstitious people, such as we know the Lycaonians at least to have been. But, at best, this is all hypothetical; there is no real evidence that Paul's trouble was ophthalmia (see on verse 15).

Be that as it may, the Galatians had not yielded to any temptations to judge the messenger, or the message that he bore, by outward appearances. They received him for what he was, God's own messenger: indeed, they received him as

---

[1] See Arndt-Gingrich under *exoutheneō*.

[2] Revelation iii. 16, which uses *emeō* 'vomit out', is much stronger, and more of the original sense is therefore kept.

they might have received Christ Himself. When Paul says *hōs angelon Theou*, *as an angel of God*, he may be referring to the treatment received at first in Lycaonia (Acts xiv. 11 ff.). It is the more appropriate in that, while grave Barnabas was taken for Zeus, the volatile and loquacious Paul was taken for Hermes, messenger of the Greek gods (though no doubt these were not the names that the Lycaonians used for their local corresponding deities). But this would depend on a South Galatian destination for the letter; while this is possible, it is safer not to make the exegesis depend upon an unproven theory.

There may be a back-reference to the 'angel from heaven' of i. 8. Paul sadly feels that once the Galatians treated him with the same exaggerated veneration that they now accord to the Judaizers. It might also refer to the constant reference that later Judaism made to the part that angels played in the mediation of the law. Paul has already referred to this in iii. 19. Time was when the Galatians received Paul's gospel as 'angel-mediated' too. Or the word might be used in a simple superlative sense, rather as we say 'a perfect angel'. That there is some sort of ascending scale we can see, from the addition of *even as Christ Jesus*. Here Paul is not going beyond the Gospel: the Lord said that he who received His messenger, received Him (Mt. x. 40).

There is always, however, the possibility that Paul is using *angelos* in its neutral sense of 'messenger'; naturally 'God's messenger' often is an angel, but unless the 'from heaven' is actually added we cannot be sure. As this is the most general sense, it is preferable. In 2 Corinthians xii. 7, Paul's 'thorn in the flesh' is described as *angelos Satanā*, 'Satan's messenger', in just such a neutral sense.

15. What Paul means by *makarismos*, *blessedness*, is not quite clear. It is obviously something once enjoyed by the Galatians but now lost. Arndt-Gingrich comes down firmly on the side of 'blessing', but glosses as 'the frame of mind in which you blessed yourselves'. NEB amplifies with 'how happy you thought yourselves in having me with you', which is undoubtedly the general thought. Perhaps 'your former happy state' is safest, leaving open the exact reason for their happiness. That it had something to do with their attitude to Paul is clear from the illustration. They would have given their very eyes to help him if they could. Those who see here a proof that Paul suffered from ophthalmia, or some similar eye-disease, are welcome to do so. Certainly with smoky fires, no chimneys, and oil lamps, one would expect a high incidence of eye trouble in the first-century Mediterranean world. To one who had spent years poring over crabbed Hebrew tomes the risk might well be greater. But again we have no proof. In most languages the eye is a symbol of the most precious possession. Both Old Testament and New Testament alike use the metaphor (Dt. xxxii. 10 and Mt. xviii. 9 are examples respectively). So there is no need to see here more than the language of extravagant devotion of convert to teacher. On other grounds, Paul's trouble would seem to have been some form of 'nervous prostration' rather than a direct physical handicap ike ophthal mia.

16. So far he has been describing their former attitude to him. Now they act as though he has become their enemy. Why is it? What has he done? This change has been brought about purely through his *alētheuōn*, 'telling the truth' to them (NEB, 'by being honest with you'). There is an implied contrast with those whose behaviour has been thoroughly dishonest, but he will speak more of them later. Ephesians iv. 15 shows what a typical Christian virtue this integrity of speech is when it is joined with, and tempered by, that other typically Christian virtue, love.

In verses 17–20 the only problem centres around the translation of *zēlousin* and kindred words. In the paraphrase, they have been uniformly translated 'envy'. This is preferred by the NEB. It is at least as possible, however, that they should be translated 'be deeply concerned about someone', 'court someone's favour' (see Arndt-Gingrich). This is favoured by NEB mg. If taken in this sense the word should be understood in the context of 2 Corinthians xi and the marriage-metaphor used there. Otherwise we shall not see what Paul means by saying that there is a 'good kind' as well as a 'bad kind' of *zēlos*. One of our difficulties in English is that 'jealousy' has not only a defined meaning, but a bad sense. Neither of these were true of Hebrew, and it is doubtful if they were true of Greek. We find it hard to see how God can be described as a 'jealous God' in Exodus xx. 5 and elsewhere. To make this intelligible to a modern congregation we often have to substitute 'zealous' which originally was merely an alternative spelling. But within marriage there is a place for an exclusive relationship, and any breach of that should arouse strong feelings of the type that Paul is describing.[1]

A very strong case, however, can be made out for 'envy'. It is quite consonant with Paul's position to say that the true psychological reason for the onslaught of the Judaizers on the Galatians is that they secretly envy the Galatians both their freedom in Christ and the spontaneity of their relations with Paul. They want to 'cut them out' from both of these and to reduce them to the pitiable state of envying the Judaizers themselves. Whether or no this is their conscious motive makes no difference; this will be the inevitable result of their preaching. It must be admitted that verse 18 is hard to explain purely in terms of 'envy' without also introducing the idea of 'pay court to'. But the answer is probably that the Greek was conscious of the two meanings side by side all the time, and could easily pass from one to the other.

17. When Paul says that the Judaizers *would exclude you* (*ekkleisai*; NEB, 'to bar the door'), he is probably thinking back to the *sunkleio* of iii. 22, 23. The law deliberately 'herded men together' as sinners so that they might find salvation; these Judaizers are 'bolting men outside' lest they should enjoy salvation. There could be no greater contrast than between the Judaizers and the very law that they profess to teach.

18–20. The second half of verse 18 is highly compressed which makes a literal translation difficult, though the sense is not in dispute. Paul means that, when he is present, the

[1] See *zēlotupos*, 'the jealous husband', in Liddell-Scott-Jones.

Galatians show plenty of this 'zeal' (of whatever kind it is); he only wishes that they showed it equally in his absence. That leads him to the thought that, if only he were with them now, he would not need to use such a severe tone (the probable meaning of *allaxai tēn phōnēn* in verse 20. See Arndt-Gingrich; but note also the NEB mg. translation 'could exchange words with you'). As it is, he confesses that he does not know what to make of them (NEB, 'I am at my wits' end'). Not even Paul himself is sure that he has taken the wisest line with these lapsed Christians; he doubtless had done so, but he was still full of misgiving.

Now, for the first time in this letter, Paul breaks through the formal barrier of *adelphoi*, 'brothers in Christ'. He calls the Galatians *tekna mou*, *my little children*; for such they were, the fruit of his labour in Christ. No word could better express the closeness of the bond that often exists between an evangelist and the church which God has used him to build. And no term is more frequently on the lips of Paul, whether it be used collectively to the Corinthians (e.g. 1 Cor. iv. 14 f.) or individually to men like Timothy, Titus, and Philemon (e.g. Phm. 10). Paul never attempts to deny the importance of 'follow-up' work (1 Cor. iii. 6), but he does assert that this earlier relationship is of a deeper and exclusive nature (1 Cor. iv. 15). His converts are his joy and crown, as well as his 'letters of introduction'; that is why he cannot bear to see them thus subverted (1 Thes. ii. 19).

But all his 'labour-pains' are not over yet; for, with a typical mixture of metaphor, Paul says he is in labour all over again 'until you take the shape of Christ' (NEB). No-one doubts his meaning. His is the agony of the pastor, watching for signs of Christian growth in his flock. Paul tells us in 2 Corinthians xi. 28 that this was the heaviest burden which he had to bear. It is therefore false to think of Paul merely as the prince of evangelists; he was also the prince of pastors.

The NEB translation quoted above makes admirable sense, and it undoubtedly rescues Paul from a difficulty: but it does not seem to be what he wrote. The *morphōthē* (*be formed*, 'shaped') has *Christos* as subject. The literal meaning can only be *until*

Christ be formed in you, as in Arndt-Gingrich, who quote Galen and others to show the use of this verb to describe the formation of the embryo in the womb before birth. If we say that this is an impossible mixture of metaphors, the answer is that, impossible or no, Paul has used it, and we all understand his meaning. He is not giving us a lecture on embryology, but an illustration of two things: first, his own care and anxiety, and second, the need for growth 'in Christ'—whether before or after 'birth' makes little difference. Honesty compels us to admit that some of Paul's illustrations from seed-sowing and grafting are equally 'impossible' in the physical world. But that does not mean that they cease to be effective illustrations. It is unnecessary to take a strong theological position and say that Paul used these illustrations just because they were impossible, and thus the only fit pictures of the working of the God of the Impossible. It is enough to say that Paul was not a gardener; nor, we may add, a mother or midwife.

h. An argument from rabbinics (iv. 21–v. 1)

Paul now uses a typically rabbinic argument. We have seen certain rabbinic elements in his use of the promise 'to Abraham's issue' in iii. 16; but this goes much further. Again, Ellis, *Paul's Use of the Old Testament* may be consulted. There are several possible reasons for his use of this type of argument here. It may be an *argumentum ad hominem*, an argument addressed strictly to the audience that he expects to listen to it. The opening words suggest this strongly. The Galatians are fascinated by rabbinic exegesis of the law, are they? Good; here then is an argument that, on their own terms, they must accept. It seems as if the Lord often dealt with His Jewish opponents along these lines before meeting their objections at a deeper level; Matthew xxii. 41–46 is perhaps an illustration of this. At times Paul certainly uses the 'language of accommodation' in theological controversy; for the sake of argument he will use his opponent's terms (and sometimes even adopt his position) just to show that it is untenable. Of course, he may always be thinking of the Judaizers rather than the Galatians. Although addressed directly to his erring converts, this argument would be even more telling as far as their new teachers were concerned.

The other main possibility is that Paul, from his long and thorough training under Gamaliel, was so steeped in rabbinics that this style of thought was congenial, and indeed natural, to him. But this is scarcely fair to Paul. It is true that he carries over into his Christian days many of the habits of thought of old Jewish days; but this was the divine preparation for his task. Moreover, such a strongly rabbinic flavour is not generally characteristic of Paul's exegesis, which has the same new freshness and directness as the rest of the new Christian 'school'. That suggests that there is a special reason for its use here, and a Jewish (or Judaized) audience is as good a guess as any. If the South Galatian theory be followed, then a not inconsiderable part of the church would have had either a Jewish or proselyte background, and such arguments would have double interest for them. In any case, it is purely the manner, not the matter, of the argument which is rabbinic; the great scriptural principles remain true, however applied.

'Tell me, do you not listen to what the law says—you who want to be under law as a system? Scripture says that Abraham had two sons, one by the slave-wife and the other by the freeborn wife. The slave-wife's son was born perfectly naturally, but the son of the freeborn wife was born in fulfilment of God's promise. All this can be seen as a symbolic picture, for these women could represent two Covenants. The first (i.e. the slave-wife) could stand for the covenant made at Mount Sinai; all her children (i.e. those under that covenant) are in spiritual bondage. That is Hagar for you. So the scriptural character "Hagar" could also stand for Mount Sinai in Arabia. Sinai stands in the same category as the Jerusalem that we know, for she is certainly in slavery, along with her "children". But the heavenly Jerusalem stands for the freeborn wife—and she is our "mother". For Scripture says:

"Be glad, you woman who is not in childbirth;
Break into a shout of triumph, you who are not in labour;
For the abandoned wife has more children
Than the wife who has her husband."

'Now you, my fellow-Christians, are children born in fulfil-ment of God's promise, like Isaac was. But just as in those days the son born in the course of nature used to bully the son born supernaturally, so it is today. But what does Scripture say to that? "Expel the slave-wife and her son; for the slave-wife's son is certainly not going to share the inheritance with the freeborn wife's son." And so my summing-up is this: We Christians are not children of the slave-wife, but of the freeborn wife. Christ has given us our freedom; stand firm, and do not allow yourselves to be harnessed again to the yoke that spells slavery.'[1]

21, 22. To Paul's apparently innocent enquiry whether they were prepared to hear and obey the law, no doubt the Galatians would have given an indignant 'yes'. After Paul's stress on their desire to come 'under law', they could hardly say other-wise. So, too, the Lord, with an innocent *oudepote anegnōte*, 'have you never read', as He quotes a familiar passage of Scripture, makes His point in Matthew xxi. 16 and other similar places.

Paul turns to the law with something of his old relish. He even begins with the time-honoured formula of citation, *gegraptai gar, for it is written,* traditionally introducing the vital proof-text.[2] But Paul's use of the law will surprise these Galatians, and possibly their teachers as well. For Paul will again appeal to Abraham, not to Moses. It is sometimes for-gotten today that when a Jew refers to the law he means Genesis as much as Leviticus or Deuteronomy. If 'Torah' be the 'instruction' of God to His people, then history, interpreted as the story of the saving acts of God, has just as much place in it as legislation. Undoubtedly, however, the Judaizers had laid more stress in Galatia on the severely ritualistic aspects of the law. This would be a flank attack.

---

[1] It is a moot point whether v. 1 belongs to this section, as a concluding verse to 'round it off', or to the next chapter, as an introduction to Paul's expostulation as to the folly of Christian circumcision. As it is clearly a 'bridge verse', however, the question is not important, and it seems more convenient to take it with what precedes rather than with what follows.

[2] *gegrammenon estin,* 'it stands written', is another such formula. Matthew iv. 10 shows the first; John ii. 17 the second.

23. As with all the stories of Genesis, there was much Jewish speculation in connection with the two sons of Abraham and the details of the story of Sarah and Hagar. This need not detain us, except to note that Paul is not choosing some obscure passage, but one which was a familiar battleground. First, Paul runs over the details of the story, with which the Galatians may not have been as familiar as he. When he says that Ishmael was born *kata sarka*, 'according to flesh', he probably limits his meaning to 'in the ordinary run of events'.[1] What he means is that no miracle was necessary, and no promise of God. Whether he is blaming Abraham for taking this secondary wife, out of lack of faith, is not certain; there is certainly a contrast between the birth 'by natural means' and the birth of Isaac 'through God's promise' (NEB). But even if he blamed Abraham for this, no Jew would object: some Rabbis so taught.

24. So far, not the most ardent Judaizer could disagree with Paul—not even when he says that these things are *allēgoroumena*, *an allegory* in the corresponding English form. Most Jews were quite ready to treat the Old Testament in this way. The only question is—What do these two women stand for allegorically? There is plenty of evidence in pagan literature for the use of this verb in the sense of 'to speak of something under other terms' (see Arndt-Gingrich). It is doubtful if Paul is using it in any highly technical sense to distinguish it from other types of 'simple' exegesis known to Jews, and later amplified by Christians. If he were, such finesse would probably be wasted on the Galatians. Nor does he wish to deny the literal truth of the story as some allegorists might do. His sole concern is to show the Galatians that, behind the plain meaning of the words, there is to be found the exemplification of a great spiritual truth. This truth, this divine principle, he finds demonstrated on a larger scale elsewhere in God's dealing with men; and he proceeds to show where this is. A little reflection will show that, since God is changeless, and these

[1] At times *sarx*, 'flesh', is used in a euphemistic sense in connection with physical generation, rather like the Hebrew *basar*, 'flesh', in the Old Testament.

spiritual principles are therefore also changeless, this is not arbitrary interpretation.

Some might object that the chief actor in the Genesis story is not God, but Abraham, and that Paul is thus arguing, not from God to God (as we might say) which is legitimate, but from Abraham to God which is illegitimate. In reply, it could be said that Abraham, in his life, exemplifies the only two possible attitudes towards God, faith and unbelief. This is the main point of the allegory, and if this be kept central, all else will fall into place. Faith and unbelief, natural and spiritual, earthly and heavenly, below and above, slavish and free— there are many pairs of opposites used in the passage, but all have this one root. It is only when Paul applies this distinction to the 'two covenants' that the Jew would sharply disagree; indeed, to the latter the very concept of the 'two covenants' was abhorrent. The 'new covenant' to him was something eschatological, yet to come, belonging to the age of the Messiah (Je. xxxi. 31). What they could not believe was that this day had come without their noticing it (cf. Lk. xi. 20, with its use of *ephthasen*, 'come upon you').

Now if we follow this line of reasoning, we can see why the Jews are compared to Ishmael and his descendants, not to Isaac. Certainly they are 'children of the covenant' (their proud claim), but they are children of the covenant made on Mount Sinai, not of that made with Abraham. Paul has already shown that to try to win salvation by keeping the law is to enter a hopeless and fruitless bondage. Yet this is the bondage inevitable to the Jew. That is why this covenant 'bears sons destined to be slaves' (NEB, 'bearing children into slavery'). This was doubly appropriate in the ancient world, for the children of a slave-wife were themselves slaves, unless the husband and master acknowledged them as true sons. Of course, it was not inevitable that the Jews should serve in this 'slavish' way. They were 'Abraham's seed' and children of the covenant with Abraham as truly as they were children of the covenant with Moses.[1] But as long as they looked on the law

---

[1] In every case, 'children' is used in the idiomatic Hebrew sense of 'sharers in'; but Paul plays on the literal sense as well.

as a possible means of salvation, such 'slavery' was inevitable. This reasoning is impeccable theologically, but it must have been a bitter pill for any Jew—all the more so because he prided himself on being Isaac's offspring, not an 'Ishmaelite' like the despised desert-dwellers of the Negev.

25. There has been much discussion on the first three words *to de Agar*, 'now then Hagar'. It is possible that they ought to be omitted altogether, as an explanatory 'gloss' on the text (so NEB). But this conjecture is not borne out by ancient witnesses. If the clause is kept, it is best explained as another back-reference to Hagar the slave-wife, as though Paul were anxious to keep us reminded of the 'corresponding terms' of the analogy. Much ingenuity has been spent by commentators, ancient and modern, in finding a reference to some generic or specific name for an actual mountain in Arabia; but if the explanation above is correct, this is ruled out of court. Even if, on the basis of Arabic, some such name could be postulated, there is no reason for Paul to introduce such a direct geographic reference. It would be utterly out of tune with the rest of the analogy.

One other reason that made commentators of the past anxious to discover a local reference here was the allusion in i. 17 to a time spent by Paul in 'Arabia' immediately after his conversion. But it is highly unlikely that this refers to anything other than the country areas in the immediate vicinity of Damascus, under the control of Aretas. There is no evidence in Scripture to suggest that Paul had any knowledge of the southern desert where Sinai was situated.

The word *sunstoichei*, 'corresponds to', 'marches with', is used primarily of soldiers 'dressing ranks'. Hence it is used of objects or ideas in 'similar categories'. Here it is not used in any highly technical sense; perhaps 'stands for' might be sufficient (NEB, 'represents'). Sometimes in this passage Paul seems to use *estin*, 'is', in the same sense of 'represents': for neither Sinai, nor the Sinaitic covenant, *is* Hagar, in the full sense of the predicate (see the end of verse 24). To remember this possibility might save much fruitless discussion over the exact meaning of the words of institution of the Lord's Supper (Mt. xxvi. 26–28).

26. When Paul contrasts *Jerusalem which now is* with *Jerusalem which is above* (or, 'the heavenly Jerusalem'), he is really mixing two metaphors but with no danger of misunderstanding. The exact contrast would be first, between the present Jerusalem and the future Jerusalem, and secondly, between Jerusalem below and Jerusalem above. The concept of a 'new Jerusalem' is very familiar from the Old Testament, especially in the days when the old, familiar city had been burnt and ravaged (see, e.g. Zc. viii. 1–8, to take a random instance). Naturally, since this was an eschatological concept, it tended to be contrasted, as future, with the miserable Jerusalem of the present. Also, in view of passages like Ezekiel xlviii and Isaiah lxii, it was easy to speak of an ideal Jerusalem already existing in heaven in the mind and purpose of God, and one day to be established on earth by the act of God. All of these thoughts find full expression in Revelation iii. 12 and xxi. 2; but these passages are really only a cento of quotations from the Old Testament. To Paul, 'the Jerusalem of today' (NEB) is not only the familiar city of his boyhood with the Temple at its heart, but also the whole race of Israel. Again, this was a familiar usage from the Old Testament where 'Jerusalem' can stand for the whole nation, especially in prophetic address. This heavenly Jerusalem *is the mother of us all*. To be her children is to have already entered this eschatological age of fulfilment of all of God's promises; and this the Christian has already done through trust in God's Messiah. This is the same stress as that in iv. 4 and elsewhere with its concept of 'the fulness of time'. God's hour has struck.

27. The quotation from Isaiah liv is appropriate for many reasons, although there is no direct evidence in the original that it was ever applied to the barren Sarah. Its direct reference is to desolate Israel, and secondarily to Jerusalem (witness the architectural metaphors in Isaiah liv. 11 ff.). Since in this passage Israel is seen as the 'bride' of God, the thought of Revelation finds a ready echo. And because the Christian

Church is also seen as the 'bride of Christ' (see 2 Cor. xi. 2 for the Pauline use), a whole system of identifications comes into operation at once. To the Jew it was long familiar from prophecy that the Gentiles would turn to God in multitudes. What was a stumbling-block (or 'staggering') to him in this new Christian interpretation was that these Gentiles did not need to become Jews first. Even for an 'orthodox' Jewish Christian of the time of Paul it must have come as a shock to realize that Gentile Christians were already far outnumbering Jewish Christians—a fact which we accept without thinking. Stranger still, the time would come when the Gentile Christian Church would far outnumber unbelieving Jewry. Then indeed the words of this prophecy would find fulfilment.

28, 29. After all this, it was easy for the Christians to see that they, *as Isaac was, are the children of promise*. They knew that there was nothing 'natural' about their spiritual re-birth (cf. Jn. i. 13). But they may also have ruefully wondered why, if all this could be shown so clearly from the Torah, their Jewish 'brethren' should persecute them so. Paul has an answer to that too, again drawn from the traditional rabbinic exegesis of Genesis xxi. 9, where 'playing with' (RSV) is interpreted 'mocking at' Isaac (cf. AV). To Paul this is not only an illustration of Ishmael's probable attitude towards Isaac; it is also the actual attitude of Judaism to the Church. More, it is the inevitable reaction of all 'natural' religion to 'supernatural'. Acts xiv shows at least the sort of experience that Paul had had, at the hands of the Jews of Asia Minor.

30. Does that mean, then, that Jew and Christian are together co-heirs of God's grace? No, says Paul, returning again to his illustration. The reason why all 'natural' religious systems are bound to come into conflict with Christianity, the 'supernatural' system, is because they cannot co-exist as parallel paths to the same goal. That is why the 'persecution' mentioned above is inevitable. Christianity is incurably 'narrow-minded'. That is an unpopular doctrine today when 'conversation' with other faiths is being suggested, rather than preaching the gospel. But this is the 'severity' of God that co-exists for Paul along with His goodness (Rom. xi. 22); and it is nowhere exhibited more clearly than in God's dealings with Israel and the Church respectively. Ishmael cannot inherit along with Isaac. Jew and Gentile may and will co-exist in the Christian Church—but only as 'Isaac', not as 'Ishmael'. Unbelieving Israel is excluded from blessing.

31. After that, *dio, so then*, or 'therefore' is but a resumption of the main argument. It would be weakening Paul's position to take it in any closer sense—as though Paul were saying, 'Because Ishmael's fate is so terrible we must determine to follow Isaac.' The thought of warning may well be in his mind; it may indeed be one reason why he tells the story at all. But it is not expressed here. So we may translate with NEB, 'You see, then'.

v. 1. This verse is thoroughly Hebraic, with its 'Christ has freed us with freedom'. In translation, an emphasis of voice would be sufficient to bring out the force of the repetition, a common Semitic device. The use of the *eleutheria*, 'freedom', is certainly designed to recall the *eleuthera*, 'freeborn woman', of the allegory. But it is also intended to remind his readers, by contrast, of the possibility of slipping back into the slavery from which they have only just emerged. The *zugō douleias*, *yoke of bondage*, contains more than meets the eye. The Jew spoke of 'taking the yoke of the law' upon oneself; and it is highly likely that the Judaizers, whether from inside or outside the Church, had used this sort of language in Galatia. To Paul this was a slave's yoke, and he says so bluntly. But there may have been in his mind the memory of a saying of Christ where He contrasted such heavy burdens with the 'easy yoke' of following Him (see Mt. xi. 30). (It is also possible that we should understand the dative *eleutheria* as the goal or object: 'with a view to enjoying freedom, Christ set us free.' The emphatic position of the word might support this.)

III. THE MORAL ARGUMENT (v. 2–vi. 18)

Paul has three great lines of argument, any one of which would be incontrovertible. The combination of the three is overpowering. First, he has argued in chapters i and ii from history, from what all men knew to have taken place. His own experience and the experience of the Galatians were known to all, however some might try to explain them. Paul's relations with the Jerusalem church were an open book which all men might read. Even had Paul been capable of attempting to falsify such evidence, it would have been an impossible task. There were too many men still alive who could have contradicted him, and the Judaizers would have been the very first to seize upon any inconsistency.

Secondly, he has argued in chapters iii and iv from theology, or rather from Scripture. Both from 'general' and from 'special' (rabbinic) exegesis, he has shown the utter inconsistency of the theological position of the Judaizers and Galatians alike. He has established beyond doubt that such retrograde teaching is contradicted by the very Torah which they claimed to teach. Promise and fulfilment meet in the Christian Church.

But there still remains one very powerful argument—some would say the most powerful of all. This is the moral argument, the appeal to the total inward moral change brought about by the 'freedom' of the gospel, a change which all the restraints of the Jewish law had utterly failed to produce. In these last two chapters Paul will hammer this home in order to clinch the matter. But he does not merely have the Judaizers in mind when he stresses the moral obligations and fruits of the gospel; he also does it lest his preaching of 'freedom' be misinterpreted as 'antinomianism' by the Galatians. If liberty becomes licence, then the worst suspicions of the Judaizers would be true and the last state of the Galatians worse than the first. From every point of view, therefore, these chapters are the crown of the book.

a. The goal of the gospel (v. 2–6)

At first sight this short section may look like a simple attack on the Judaizers for their preaching of circumcision, but it goes far beyond that. It is an exposition of the true end of law and gospel alike, and of the impotence of any outward observance to effect that which can only be achieved by the working of the Spirit. The true centre of gravity of the passage lies in the last clause.

'Look, I Paul, in person, tell you this: if you should now accept circumcision, Christ will be no good to you. I affirm solemnly again to every man who accepts circumcision that he is thereby accepting an obligation to carry out the whole of the law. Seeing that you are trying to obtain right standing with God through obeying the law, you have broken the bond (sc. "of faith") that united you to Christ; you have slipped from the level where grace operates. For we Christians wait eagerly for that righteousness which we expect as a result of faith; and all is the Spirit's doing. Once a man's faith is placed in Christ, neither circumcision nor uncircumcision is any good; the only thing that counts is faith, working out in love (NEB mg., "faith inspired by love")'.

2. When Paul bursts into this passionate personal testimony, one wonders whether he has also snatched the stylus from the hand of the scribe and is writing it in his own handwriting. It resembles the opening formula with which he introduces autograph passages elsewhere (as in 1 Cor. xvi. 21). 2 Thessalonians iii. 17 tells us that this autographing was his invariable practice to guard against forgery. So we may assume that wherever 'the Grace' occurs at the end of an Epistle, it was originally in autograph, even if not specifically stated in the context. But there is no reference here to handwriting at all; for that we must wait until vi. 11. It therefore seems unlikely that Paul picked up the pen so early in the letter unless, as is always possible, he wrote this letter without the aid of an amanuensis. That would make the reference in vi. 11 to the size and shape of the letters more understandable; for Paul does not normally write more than 'the Grace' in his own hand, and this will not come until vi. 18. What exactly, then, is the force of the *I Paul*? Perhaps it is only to lend force to the solemn affirmation which follows. When Paul says, in the next verse, *marturomai, I testify*, his words take on the character of a declaration under oath in a court of law. Paul's lawyer's training, apart altogether from his Jewish background, would not allow him to use such a phrase lightly. Normally in his Epistles such an introduction marks a point of more than usual weight and moment.

That may well be the explanation of the phrase here. But it is also possible that the words are pregnant with further meaning. Even Paul, the circumcised Jew, proud of all his background and traditions (cf. Phil. iii. 4-6), tells them that circumcision is of no avail. Who more than he should know its value? Yet he had counted it as 'debit', as 'refuse', in comparison with Christ. Paul is never anti-Jewish even when he is in his most controversial moods. Although he does not develop in Galatians the positive values and abiding contribution of Judaism, Romans ix–xi shows his general position clearly. Israel never had a man who loved her more dearly than Paul—unless it was Jesus of Nazareth (see Lk. xix. 41). Yet even such a Jewish patriot sees clearly the comparative unimportance of circumcision.

The tenses of the verbs are very important in this passage. Paul says to the Galatians 'if you should get yourselves circumcised', *ean peritemnēsthe*. This implies that they have not already taken the step but are considering it. It also means that Paul is in no way condemning those Jewish Christians who are in any case already circumcised. He does not say 'if you are in the position of circumcised men' (which would normally require the Perfect Passive). To such, Paul's advice is quite clear in 1 Corinthians vii. 17–20, where it is set in a wider context. If God's call came to a man while he was a Jew, and therefore circumcised, then 'let him not seek to remove the marks of circumcision' (as some Jews did in time of persecution; cf. 1 Macc. i. 15). If the call came while he was a Gentile, and therefore uncircumcised, then 'let him not seek circumcision' (both translations from RSV). Paul in no way condemned the usages of the Jerusalem church. That is an important point for he was often accused by his Judaizing foes of doing this (e.g. Acts xxi. 21). What he did condemn was the attitude of mind that saw such usages as necessary to salvation and which tried to force them on Gentile churches as the price of fellowship at the Lord's Table. This is an attitude of mind that the Church of the twentieth century has not yet outgrown. We cannot afford to smile at the Judaizers if we too 'Judaize'.

That this force of the verb is not imaginary is shown by *peritemnomenō*, in the next verse, 'becoming circumcised at this moment', where the present tense is likewise used. It is not unfair to translate as 'trying to be circumcised' or 'wanting to be circumcised'; there are places in the New Testament where the present participle has both of these nuances. Hence the urgency of this letter. Paul may be able to stop the Galatians from what in his opinion would be an irrevocable and retrograde step.

To say 'Christ will be no good to you', *ouden ōphelēsei*, is to use a very strong expression. But, once again, Paul wants to shock the Galatians into a full realization of what they might have done. He will explain what he means in the following verses. Meanwhile, we may note the untranslatable pun between *ōphelēsei*, 'helps, benefits', and *opheiletēs*, 'debtor', in the next verse. It is somewhat of a bitter pun, but it heightens the contrast. We might attempt to bring out the force by saying, 'So far from Christ helping you, you yourself will be helpless in law's clutches'.

3, 4. Paul's point is quite clear. If the Galatians accept circumcision, it must be because they consider that circumcision is necessary to salvation. This would mean that Christ's death was not enough, and they are not trusting Christ to save them. Rather, they are hoping to save themselves by what they do. Thus they have in fact left the region where grace is operative; *tēs charitos exepesate*, 'you have fallen out of grace' (not the same as colloquial English, 'you have fallen from grace'). No man can be justified in two ways at once; he cannot be justified by faith in Christ and by his own efforts. It is 'all or nothing' as far as faith and grace are concerned.

Paul probably could have proved this even if the Judaizers were insisting only on the one rite of circumcision. But iv. 10 shows that the whole gamut of Jewish festivals was also involved, and ii. 12 makes it highly probable that the Jewish food-laws were included. For while to Paul circumcision is primarily the 'seal' of God on the faith of Abraham (iii. 11) and an assurance of that righteousness which was already his by faith, to the Jew of Paul's day circumcision was something fundamentally different. To him it was the first act of obedience to that law which would henceforth, if he was a pious Jew, rule every tiny detail of his life. Through complete obedience to all its precepts he hoped to win merit in God's eyes, and thus attain 'life'. Circumcision, in Jewish eyes, was therefore more closely associated with Moses and Sinai than with Abraham and the Promised Land. Thus Paul is right when he says that to accept circumcision as obligatory is to accept *the whole law* as obligatory. This is a world other than that of Christ.

So he can say, 'you are severed, *katērgēthēte*, from Christ' (RSV). The vital bond of faith in God's grace has been broken, and no other relationship with Christ is possible for the Christian. It is true that this Greek verb can mean 'make ineffective, nullify' in a general sense (see Arndt-Gingrich). But Paul uses it in Romans vii. 2 in the sense of 'be freed from a marriage-bond', and that is a most suitable meaning here too. So NEB translates, 'your relation with Christ is completely severed'.

5. As against this we now find one of the clearest statements of 'justification by faith' in the whole Epistle. The initial *hēmeis*, 'we' is so strongly adversative that it is not incorrect to interpret it as 'we Christians'. It may be that Paul uses the plural deliberately here, as though to include the wavering Galatians with himself. But this use of plural for singular is common enough throughout the whole New Testament. The meaning 'eagerly wait for' seems established for *apekdechometha*: (see Arndt-Gingrich); otherwise it would be tempting to translate 'we receive payment in full' with a future reference. There is a future aspect in any case, implied not only by the verb but also by the phrase *elpida dikaiosunēs*, lit. *hope of righteousness*. But this does not mean that, to Paul, 'justification' is something still to come, and thus something uncertain as yet. He uses the past tense too often to admit that.[1] Instead of *hope of righteousness* we should probably translate 'that righteousness which we expect', for there is nothing uncertain about *elpis*, 'hope', in the Bible. In that case, Paul will either be referring to the continual attitude of the Christian, which is a buoyant expectation that God is in fact accepting him as 'in the right'; or there may be a slight eschatological flavour— as though the Christian were waiting confidently for that 'right standing' to be manifested to all. He was a wise theologian who said that, in the Bible, salvation is at the same time past, present, and future: we have been saved, we are being saved, and we shall be saved: and yet there is no contradiction between these three.

But the weight of the verse, as far as Paul is concerned, does not fall on the second half, interesting though it may be to us. The whole stress is on the words that he has deliberately brought forward for emphasis: *pneumati*, 'by Spirit', and *ek pisteōs*, 'as a result of faith'. These are the two aspects that distinguish the Christian hope from the Jewish, for here the two approaches to God are poles apart. If circumcision was anything, it was *sarki*, 'in the flesh'; and although Paul does not use the word here, it can hardly be absent from his mind. To the Christian, justification has nothing to do with anything 'fleshly' or 'natural'; all is of God; all is 'the work of the Spirit' (NEB). Paul may simply wish to contrast a 'spiritual' with a 'natural' method. Or, as the NEB translation suggests, he may be emphasizing that, from start to finish, this is due to the work of the Spirit. This need not have direct reference to the work of the Spirit in 'sanctification'; it is equally by the work of the Spirit that we are convinced of the impossibility of commending ourselves to God by our own activities (whether by obedience to the Jewish law, in the case of Jews, or obedience to the dictates of conscience, in the case of Gentiles). Further, it is by the work of the Spirit that we see Christ as our Saviour.

[1] e.g. Romans v. 1, etc., *dikaiōthentes*, 'having been justified'.

Indeed, it might almost be said that the gift of faith is the first gift of the Spirit to the newborn soul.

After the explosive *pneumati*, 'by the Spirit', comes the almost equally emphatic *ek pisteōs*, 'as a result of faith'. What this means to the Christian has already been shown in the Epistle. Here it is clearly and decisively contrasted with *en nomō*, 'by law', in the verse immediately above. Between these two there can be no truck.

6. It is part of the greatness of Paul that even in the midst of controversy he is not one-sided. Just as in i. 18 he readily admits that he did actually once go to Jerusalem 'to see Peter' (although knowing that this admission might well weaken and damage his case), so here he is not content to prove that circumcision 'does no good' (unless *ischuei* should be translated 'makes no difference', with NEB). He equally admits that uncircumcision is valueless too—a point often forgotten by those filled with reforming zeal as it was probably forgotten by many a Gentile Christian. He will not allow the Gentile to boast of his uncircumcised state, any more than he will allow the Jew to boast of 'the sign of the covenant'. Both states are now irrelevant 'in Christ'.

We might perhaps compare the brief way in which he dismisses the Corinthian food-problem in 1 Corinthians viii. 8: 'Food will not commend us to God. We are no worse off if we do not eat, and no better off if we do' (RSV). This is a noble perspective which might have saved the Church of yesterday and today many a quarrel, much heartburning, and not a little criticism. To him, these outward observances are all unimportant compared with *faith which worketh by love* (unless *energoumenē* is to be taken as a full passive, in which case the NEB mg. 'faith inspired by love' might possibly be correct). Again, we might compare the explosive dismissal of a similar subject in Romans xiv. 17, 'For the kingdom of God does not mean food and drink but righteousness and peace and joy in the Holy Spirit' (RSV).

Either translation of *energoumenē*, 'working out' or 'being worked out', is good sense. For it is the love of Christ which moves our hearts to response in Him; therefore it is true to say that our faith is 'inspired by love' (NEB mg.). But it is more usual in the New Testament to say that Christ's love evokes a corresponding love in us (1 Jn. iv. 19) than to say that our faith actually stems from love. Those who say that 'love' in John virtually corresponds to 'faith' in Paul will judge otherwise; but it seems as if the NEB text (not margin), 'faith active in love', is nearer the mark. This would link with two favourite Pauline thoughts: first, that love is the fulfilment of the law (Rom. xiii. 10), and secondly, that Christian faith brings with it, as corollary, the 'fruit of the Spirit'. The first is necessary to show that there is no opposition between the sort of 'righteousness' that the law seeks vainly to produce and that which is the free gift of God in response to faith. The second is necessary to show that the faith through which we are justified is not barren intellectual understanding. No man soberly reading the rest of the Epistle could seriously say that there is any conflict between James and Paul on the nature of faith; any apparent contradiction is superficial and verbal only. Whether of course this was equally plain to James, we cannot tell; but certainly he recognized the Pauline gospel as the same as his own.

b. A personal aside (v. 7–12)

Paul, on 'faith that works out through love', has set the tone for the whole of this last section of the Epistle. But in the next few verses he turns aside for another personal expostulation directed at the Galatians. It is not without interest, both with the reference to the 'enemy' at Galatia and also with reference to Paul's own personal position.

'You were running strongly: who was it who thwarted you, by stopping you from believing the truth? This sort of persuasiveness never came from the God who called you; "a little pinch of yeast sets the whole lump of dough in fermentation". But I have a Christian confidence as far as you are concerned that you will not change your outlook. This disturber of your peace will bear his judgment, no matter how high his position. But I ask you, fellow-Christians, If I am one who proclaims the need of circumcision, why am I still being harried from place to place? The stumbling-block of the cross would be gone then. Oh, if only those who trouble you would go and mutilate themselves!'

7. The metaphor in *etrechete, you did run*, is from the running track that dominated the Greek athletic world. No orthodox Jew could or would join in such an exercise since it involved nudity as well as perfunctory worship of heathen gods. The pictures that we draw of Paul attending athletic games at Tarsus as a boy are therefore probably figments of our imagination (unless Paul, like other naughty small boys, disobeyed his parents). But the imagery of the arena fascinated him. See 1 Corinthians ix. 24–27 for just one instance of it. Perhaps here there is a deliberate reminiscence of ii. 2, where Paul explains to the Jerusalem elders the gospel that he preaches 'lest all my running be in vain'. The figurative use of this verb with reference to moral effort is very common throughout the whole New Testament.

If the metaphor be still strongly felt, it is tempting to take *enekopsen, hinder*, as a reference to 'foul running' by rivals, and translate 'edged you off the track' (cf. Phillips, 'put you off the course'). But although meanings like 'knock in' are found there is no evidence to justify such an interpretation. It is probably better to take it simply as 'obstructed', 'hindered', and assume that the force of the metaphor has weakened already. When Paul says that the purpose (or perhaps result) of this 'hindering' was that the Galatians might *not obey the truth*, he uses the infinitive *peithesthai*, 'to be persuaded'. The meaning is quite clear. This Judaizing approach has turned the Galatians away from following the plain truth of the gospel, whether they know it or not.

8. The choice of this particular verb allows him a play on words hard to reproduce in English, for the verb is now taken up by the cognate noun *peismonē*, 'persuasion', 'persuasiveness', used to describe the activity of the Judaizers. While Paul does not actually say here that they are plausible deceivers (which he has already hinted in iv. 17), the deduction is obvious.

Those who translate 'obedience' (referring to the ready response of the Galatians rather than to the proselytizing activity of the Judaizers) must depart from the best text for the passage (see Arndt-Gingrich). In either case, the play on words remains: and it is taken up by the *pepoiiha*, 'I believe, I trust', in verse 10. Perhaps, at the risk of clumsiness, we might translate as: 'Who hindered you from being persuaded as to the truth? The sort of "persuasion" that they used. . . . But I am still persuaded better things of you.' The effect is to give the whole passage a coherence that it lacks in an English translation. *tou kalountos*, *him that calleth you*, is always God in Pauline theology; it cannot be used of the human evangelist, necessary though his work may be. See also note on i. 15.

9. The NEB is almost certainly right in putting verse 9 in quotation marks. It seems to be an example of Paul's use of a proverbial saying, one which he also quotes in 1 Corinthians v. 6. See Arndt-Gingrich for remarks on the phrase, which 'serves to picture the influence of apparently insignificant factors in the moral and spiritual sphere'. *Zumē*, 'yeast', is very frequently used in the Gospels, both as a symbol of the pervasiveness of evil (as here) and the pervasiveness of good (as in Mt. xiii. 33, though not all expositors are agreed there). It is highly probable that the Lord knew of this proverbial saying and it is possible that He alludes to it on several occasions. But it is not necessary to assume that the proverb itself is a dominical saying, nor even that Paul knew of the Lord's use of it. A common Jewish source is sufficient to explain the similarities. Such a proverbial usage was particularly congenial to Israel, for whom the use of 'leaven' or 'yeast' was forbidden in sacrifice (see Ex. xxxiv. 25 and many other places in the Torah). Not only so, but on certain ceremonial occasions, such as the Feast of Unleavened Bread (which immediately followed Passover), the removal of all leaven from the house had become a solemn ritual (1 Cor. v. 7, 8). While this may have served the hygienic purpose of ensuring that the whole process of breadmaking began again *de novo* at least once a year (by the creation of fresh 'leaven' from natural sources), to the Jews this was a symbol of the putting-away of sin. It is probable that the reason for the prohibition of the use of leaven in sacrifice came from an analogy between the 'leavening' activity of yeast whereby the bread 'rises', and the natural process of putrefaction. No carrion or decayed flesh might be offered to the Lord, just as no maimed or imperfect beast might be used in sacrifice (Lv. xxii. 21–25).

The *phurama*, *lump*, is the shapeless mass of the batch of dough; it literally means 'that which is mixed or kneaded' (see Arndt-Gingrich). It can also be used as in Romans ix. 21 of the formless lump of clay which the potter takes up in his hand to mould into a clay vessel. To Paul (as to Jeremiah; see chapter xviii) this shapeless mass stands for unformed human nature, whether considered in the individual (as in Romans) or in the aggregate (as here).

10. Here we are faced with the usual questions as to the force and meaning of *en Kuriō*, 'in the Lord' which for the Christian was equivalent to *en Christō*, 'in Christ'. Without trying to go into the full theological complexities of this expression we may note that there are two main possibilities. The first, and simpler, is that Paul means that this confidence of his is no human confidence, but one wrought in his heart by Jesus Christ. This is a straightforward explanation which would suit both the context in particular and Pauline theology in general. The second, and perhaps more attractive, is to translate 'united with you in the Lord' (so NEB). This is part of the modern trend to translate *en Christō*, 'in Christ', as 'in union with Jesus Christ', whether such be seen as an individual or a collective relationship. It is possibly because of this slight difficulty in interpretation that some early witnesses to the text omit the words altogether. Paul's confidence in the Galatians is that they will *ouden allo phronēsete, be none otherwise minded*. There is no difficulty with *phroneō*, 'think': it is often used of attitudes or habits of mind. Philippians ii. 5 is the classic example, but it is only one among many. But we may well ask the meaning of *allo*, 'different'. Different from what? Paul's gospel? or their original attitude? or what he has just said?

The answer is that, although the wording may be a trifle loose, there is no conflict: these three are one. NEB paraphrases well as 'you will not take the wrong view'.

Again, *ho tarassōn*, 'the troubler', is the vague character behind the scenes, whether known or unknown by name to Paul. He is the one referred to by an indignant *tis*, 'who?', in verse 7 immediately above, and also in iii. 1. The use of the singular for the plural may only be a rhetorical device; on the other hand, even if there were several Judaizers, there is certain to have been some one ringleader among them. The verb *tarassō*, 'I trouble', represents the complete antithesis of that sense of peace, coming from right relationships with God, which should be the characteristic mark of the Christian, no matter what his outward circumstances. So, in John xiv. 27, the Lord tells His disciples, 'Peace I leave with you . . . Let not your heart be troubled.'

Paul may not know who this ringleader is, but he seems to suspect that he holds high position—possibly in the Jerusalem church. That is the meaning of *hostis ean ē*, RSV, 'whoever he is'; it does not so much refer to Paul's ignorance of his identity as allude to his rank. (NEB takes a neutral position with 'whoever he may be'.) Perhaps the use of *hopoioi*, 'no matter who', in ii. 6 has a similar sense, though Paul is certainly not accusing any of the Jerusalem 'apostles' of having a direct hand in Galatian affairs.

Anyway, says Paul, such a man must *bear his judgment*. Because the Greek is *to krima*, 'the judgment', NEB is undoubtedly right in glossing as 'God's judgement'. Paul is thinking, not of a church court at Jerusalem, but of the day when all evangelists and teachers alike give account before God (cf. 1 Cor. iii. 10–15). The word *bastasei, shall bear*, is interesting. It is the very word used in Luke xiv. 27 of Christ, carrying His cross to Golgotha. There can hardly be any echo of this; but the word is also used in Acts xv. 10, in the impatient speech of Peter which turns the scale at the Jerusalem discussions. Here the law is a *zugon*, 'yoke' (cf. Gal. v. 1), which no Jew, past or present, has been able *bastasai*, 'to bear' (or possibly, 'to endure'). If the Epistle to the Galatians was written after the Council, it is conceivable that Paul is referring to, or at least remembering, Peter's words. But, if so, it is strange that he makes no reference to the so-called 'decrees' of the Council (Acts xv. 23–29). If Paul echoes Peter, he is altering the sense. Do the Judaizers want to make the new converts carry the heavy burden and yoke of the law? Let them beware. In the day of judgment they themselves will bear the far heavier burden of the wrath of God. But it is better to see both Peter and Paul referring to what were Christian commonplaces (at least among Gentiles and possibly 'Hellenists') rather than to see any direct or indirect dependence.

11. The great question here is whether anyone seriously claimed that Paul advocated circumcision. If so, who was it? When he says, 'if I am still advocating circumcision' (NEB), he may mean only 'if I were advocating it—which everybody knows that I do not'. This is certainly the simplest explanation. It is made more likely by the use of *kērussō*, 'herald abroad' (AV, *preach*; translated 'advocating' above). This, in Paul's writings, is the typical verb used for the initial preaching of the gospel (cf. ii. 2). No man could seriously think that circumcision had any place in Paul's initial proclamation of Christ. As he says himself, if only he would allow circumcision such a place, then the Judaizers would cease to harry him from pillar to post (*diōkomai, suffer persecution*, is the very word that Paul used to describe his own bitter attacks on the Church in his pre-Christian days; see i. 13). Indeed, as far as the Jews were concerned, this would remove the *skandalon*, the 'stumbling-block', from the gospel. None of them would mind Jesus Christ being added to the law: but the 'either/or' of Christian preaching was an impossible obstacle in their eyes.

Some ancient witnesses to the text omit the *eti*, 'still'. That would make the sentence run more smoothly: 'If I am a circumcision-preacher, then . . .' But such smoothness makes us suspicious that the difficult word was deliberately cut out. It may be that, if kept, it refers to Paul's pre-Christian days when he would most certainly have preached circumcision and the law with all his might. 'I preached it then,' he says;

'but not now.' It can scarcely be claimed that in his early days of gospel-preaching Paul found a greater place for the Jewish law and its observances in his gospel, for we have seen that the lines of Paul's preaching had hardened very early. Besides, such behaviour would have meant an avoidance of conflict in those early days with Jew and Judaizer, and this we see from Acts to have been untrue. Jewish riots follow Paul across Asia Minor like a trail of bushfires. There never seems to have been any such halcyonic period as that postulated by this theory. It may be, of course, that the Judaizers pointed back to the time when Paul had been willing to circumcise Timothy (Acts xvi. 3) and, just possibly, even Titus (see discussion on Gal. ii. 3). They may have told the Galatians that, in those days, even Paul had preached circumcision. But, even if they did, Paul's indignation in ii. 1–5 shows that he himself would not admit for one moment the truth of such a charge. Whatever the meaning of 'still', it cannot therefore be explained thus. Probably it is to be taken in a weak sense as 'at the present moment', with no sense of contrast with a past period.

The *offence of the cross*, *skandalon tou staurou*, 'the staggering nature of the cross', is a fundamental concept in Pauline theology and therefore demands consideration. In the Greek Old Testament, *skandalon* means a 'trap' or 'snare', and is used in parallelism with other words of the same meaning. In the New Testament, the word is frequently used of some 'temptation to sin', that which causes a man to fall. But the typical use is when it means, as here, 'that which causes revulsion, arouses opposition' (Arndt-Gingrich). 1 Corinthians i. 23 says in blunt terms that the very preaching of a crucified Messiah is a 'stumbling-block' to the religiously-minded Jew— as it is sheer nonsense to the intellectually enquiring Gentile. There is a slight difference here in that Paul is not thinking of the fact of the Messiah dying a death of shame; rather, he is stressing that this way of salvation leaves no room for 'merit' to be acquired by outward observances such as circumcision. Ultimately, of course, the two come to the same thing. For the nature of the Messiahship and the nature of the salvation that He brings are inextricably linked. Further, if salvation is to be altogether of grace, with nothing of merit, it is inevitable that both Gentile and Jew will find it a 'stumbling-block', because it is not a human way of salvation, but a divine. It is thus unavoidable that 'natural man' should find God's way of salvation 'staggering', transcending his natural powers of comprehension and acceptance. Only by the gift of God's Spirit can that which was once a 'trap' to him become his greatest boast and glory (Gal. vi. 14). Thus, whether we describe the cross itself as the 'stumbling-block', or the Lord who died upon that cross (Rom. ix. 33) it makes little difference. Paul has once again used here *katērgētai* 'has been made ineffective' as in verse 4. In its different senses it is a favourite verb with him. NEB with 'is no more' is hardly a strong enough translation.

12. Here we have Paul's final rejoinder to the Jews. If they are so enthusiastic about one 'mutilation' of the flesh (circumcision), why not go the whole way and castrate themselves— as did the eunuch priests of Asia Minor in honour of their strange, barbarous gods? That is the only possible meaning of *apokopsontai*, 'cut themselves off'. The language is strong, but it is not a coarse jest. It is designed to set circumcision in its true light as one of many ritual cuttings and markings practised in the ancient world. True, God had once used this as 'sign of covenant' in Israel; but, since He was not now using it in the Christian Church, it had no more relevance to the Gentile Christian than any other of these strange customs. Indeed, the eunuch priests of paganism undoubtedly thought that they were acquiring great 'merit' by their action. In this sense at least, therefore, there is a real comparison. Whether the Galatians lived in the north or in the south of the Roman province, they could not fail to be familiar with these cultic practices; the point would not be lost on them.

Even the Lord seems to allude to the fact that circumcision is, in one sense, a 'marring' of the human body. For He contrasts the conflicting attitudes of those who would 'break sabbath' to circumcise, yet condemn Him because He makes a man 'perfectly whole' on the sabbath (Jn. vii. 22, 23). In the original rite, this 'marring' is necessary to symbolize the 'putting away' of those things inconsistent with the following of God (Col. ii. 11). For the Christian, the true 'circumcision' is that of the heart (Rom. ii. 29); even in Old Testament times this had been seen to be equally true of Jews (see Je. vi. 10 with Acts vii. 51).

In Philippians iii. 2 Paul uses very strong language of these Judaizers. They are 'dogs' in very truth (unlike the Gentiles whom they so describe); they are 'evil workers' in spite of all their reliance on 'good deeds'; they are 'choppers', 'mutilators' (*tēn katatomēn* 'the mutilation', not *tēn peritomēn*, 'the circumcision', which is the regular term for Jews). Paul's thought there is the same as in the passage immediately before us, though it is not expressed so fully, for circumcision is described as 'mutilation'. It was because the Roman emperors confused the two practices that they issued such stringent decrees later, forbidding Jewish circumcision.

c. The true use of freedom (v. 13–18)

In this Epistle Paul has already dealt with the question of Christian freedom on several occasions (cf. v. 1). Now he will describe its right use and limitations. This is partly to show, no doubt, how the new rule of love (bound up with this freedom in Christ) is the true fulfilment of the law. It is also, perhaps, partly to forestall the usual objections by the Judaizers as to the antinomian tendencies of Pauline teaching. But one suspects that another reason for its introduction here may be the state of local church life in Galatia. Paul seems to have pretty accurate information as to the local church (iv. 10), and he may well have heard of a state of affairs that was anything but glorifying to Christian 'liberty'. It seems as if the church of Galatia was just as much rent by party factions as that of Corinth (cf. 1 Cor. i. 10–13). True, we do not know of the names or natures of the parties in Galatia; but if we may hazard a guess from what we know from the Epistle, and also from the analogy of Corinth, there was probably a Paul-party. If there had not been, it is hard to see how Paul would ever have heard of the new tendencies there. Also there must clearly have been a large majority party that favoured the Judaizers; indeed the ringleader in this movement may not have come from outside the church at all, but from within. Then, to judge from the passage before us, there may also have been a third 'Gentile' party, glorifying in their 'liberty', which to them was licence for unlimited self-indulgence. Paul did not want the support of such a group, and he may therefore have been fighting a three-cornered battle in Galatia as in other places. In any case, whether there did exist this sort of 'libertine' group (prototype of one flank of the later Gnostic movement) or no, it is obvious that party feeling ran high in Galatia, and Paul would not condone that, not even in the name of gospel truth. If this third group existed, they may have accused even Paul of 'Judaizing' tendencies in their zeal for complete Christian emancipation: to such, even Timothy's circumcision might have seemed a betrayal. It is just possible that v. 11 might have some reference to their supposed position; but this again is pure hypothesis. Any theory that makes Paul himself a Judaizer is clearly wrong-headed.

'Yes, fellow-Christians, you have been called by God with a view to freedom—only not a freedom which is a bridgehead for animal nature; instead, be willing slaves of one another for love's sake. For the whole of the law stands summed-up in this one saying, "You are to love your fellow-man as you love yourself." But if you are continually snapping at one another and eating one another alive, take care that you do not annihilate each other. What I mean is this: let your way of life be Spirit-controlled, and you will not do that for which your natural self yearns. For the yearnings of the natural self are opposed to the Spirit, and the yearnings of the Spirit are opposed to the natural self. This is because the two are utterly opposed to each other, so that you cannot do the sort of things that you want to do. But if you are continually being guided by the Spirit, then you are not under law as a system.'

13. This verse reminds us of v. 1: 'Christ set us free, to be free men' (NEB text; NEB mg., 'What Christ has done is to set us free'). True, says Paul; the goal of the divine calling (*kaleō*, 'call', always implying this divine activity) is indeed such freedom. But it must not become *aphormēn tē sarki*, 'a bridgehead for the flesh'. *Aphormē* means originally 'the starting point or base of operations for an expedition'; hence 'springboard' would be another possible translation. In 2 Corinthians xi. 12 it clearly means 'pretext', and perhaps that is the meaning here: those who shout 'Liberty' loudest in Galatia may have their tongues in their cheeks. It may however be quite neutral in meaning. Thus AV renders *occasion*, and RSV 'opportunity' (see Arndt-Gingrich).

Paul's use of *sarx, flesh*, usually as opposed to *pneuma*, 'spirit', is important and characteristic. Many individual studies have been made of both words for which any of the standard Bible Wordbooks may be consulted.[1] In brief, *sarx* begins by meaning the physical substance 'flesh', like the Hebrew *basar* which it translates in the Greek Old Testament (see Abbott-Smith). From that it means either 'body', as substance (although the word for this is more properly *sōma*), or 'mortal man'. From that, it is an easy transition to 'that which is natural to mortal man' or 'human nature'. It could be argued that this is not necessarily wrong in itself (just as *sōma*, 'body', is not wrong or sinful in itself). But there are two aspects in which it is inadequate, if not actually sinful. The first is that, when we say 'human', we now mean 'fallen human'. This is inevitable, for we have no knowledge, gained from experience, of the behaviour-patterns of unfallen man. Thus, in so far as *sarx* is the 'flesh' of fallen man, it is sinful.

Secondly, at a deeper level than this, even if we could concede that 'flesh' was once sinless and that its 'nature' was once 'unfallen nature', it is still grossly inadequate. God is spirit, and not flesh (Is. xxxi. 3); His thoughts and plans are as far above men's thoughts as heaven is above earth (Is. lv. 9). That is why God's ways are always a stumbling-block to man. That is why it is possible for there to be the 'offence of the cross'. That, in turn, is what Paul means by saying that his

---

[1] Of the older editors, Appendix XVII in Burton, entitled '*Pneuma* and *Sarx*', is one of the most useful. Among modern treatments, that of Arndt-Gingrich under the two words is excellent.

gospel is 'by revelation' (Gal. i. 12). Without the illuminating gift of God's Spirit no man can even 'see' the kingdom of God (Jn. iii. 3). As this aspect more properly falls under the heading of *pneuma*, 'spirit', it need not be further pursued here.

When Paul says we must not use (or abuse) our Christian liberty as a 'springboard for the flesh', he means 'you must not use this as an opportunity to show what man is really like'. We may translate 'lower nature' (NEB) or 'animal nature' to make the meaning clearer; but to Paul, all human nature is this 'lower nature'. We can see from the list of vices below that, while he certainly includes the grosser vices of the body in his purview (and this was very necessary in a Gentile church), he also includes the subtler vices of the mind which we normally consider as 'respectable'. The law, of course, was designed to stop man from behaving in a 'natural' manner; it was equally realistic in its approach.

Paul uses *douleuete*, *serve*, 'be slaves of (one another)', very effectively as a foil to *eleutheria*, the *liberty*, which they enjoy. This is part of the paradox by which Paul himself, freed by Jesus Christ from bondage to the Jewish law, becomes a *doulos*, 'slave', of Christ, for love's sake (see Rom. i. 1 and, indeed, the opening of most other Epistles). But such service is now voluntary; the only compulsion is that of love (2 Cor. v. 14). If we seek an Old Testament analogy it is to be found in the 'freed' slave who refuses to leave the household of the master whom he loves, but chooses deliberately to remain a 'slave' for ever (Ex. xxi. 1–6). Galatians vi. 17 may possibly refer to the 'ear-marking' which was the practice on such occasions. It is true that even in the Gentile world the 'freedman' had certain obligations and duties towards his late master; but this is not such a likely analogy.

As in verse 6 faith 'worked itself out' *di' agapēs*, 'through love', so here the mutual service to which Christians are dedicated is also 'through love'; the echo must be intentional. Some early witnesses to the text read 'through the love of the Spirit'. This, although quite correct theologically, reads like an explanatory addition, and was probably not part of the original text.

For *agapē*, 'love', see Burton, Appendix XXI, among the earlier editors. There has been much discussion in recent years of the distinction between *agapē*, seen as 'unselfish, self-giving, outgoing love', and *erōs*, seen as 'selfish, acquisitive, centripetal love'. As far as the New Testament itself is concerned, the discussion is largely academic; *erōs* is nowhere used therein, while even the 'love for the world' which is condemned in 1 John ii. 15 is described by the related verb *agapaō*. (There is also, of course, another 'love for the world', described in Jn. iii. 16, which is both right and divine and which uses the same verb.) Indeed, in pagan literature, *agapaō* may be used of sexual passion (see Moulton and Milligan). The probable truth is that *erōs* was archaic, and virtually displaced by the other word.[1] Yet since for the Christian the norm of love is the love of God and such love is free from all the human limitations mentioned above, we may justly interpret it on a higher plane. By a further extension of meaning, *agapē* came to mean the 'love-feast' of the Early Church (Jude 12).

14. When Paul says that *all the law is fulfilled*, *peplērōtai*, 'has reached its climax', 'has reached its end', he is probably punning upon two of the meanings of this Greek word. First, he means that the content of the whole law 'can be summed up' in the great words of Leviticus xix. 18. This was a commonplace of Jewish theology, for which great rabbinic names could be quoted. Matthew vii. 12 is virtually a variation on this theme, and in Matthew xxii. 39, 40 the Lord quotes this very verse from Leviticus. Again, it is not necessary to assume direct dependence (although such is always possible); probably we simply have a common source in Jewish teaching which thus receives the Lord's (and Paul's) seal of approval.

But, apart from the aspect of Leviticus xix. 18 being a useful 'summary' of the law, Paul wants to show that Christian love is actually the 'fulfilment', i.e. the 'carrying-out', of the law. See Romans xiii. 8–10 where this is worked out in detail. This is the answer both to the criticisms of the Judaizers and

[1] See the long article in Arndt-Gingrich, quoting an unquestionably pagan use of *agapē*.

the scandalous living of some of the Gentile converts, not to mention their present party-spirit.

Nomos, *law*, is in this instance the Jewish Torah with which Paul and his opponents are most directly concerned. There are, as we have seen, many places where he uses it in a wider sense, of 'law' as a system of restraints, or as a possible means of commending ourselves to God. (See Burton, Appendix XIV.) Because *torah* in Hebrew and *nomos* in Greek are far wider than the English word 'law', we have tended to lose something of the richness of the meaning. *Torah*, roughly speaking, means 'instruction'; while *nomos* covers 'customary law', and even 'customs'. Nevertheless, in view of the list of virtues and vices which follows, Paul seems to be thinking of the law here in terms of a series of injunctions, which is the usual English understanding of the word. Arndt-Gingrich suggests 'Jewish religion' as a possible translation whenever the definite article is used; this has much to commend it.

15. *daknete*, *bite*, is primarily used of snakes and animals; it is so employed even in Hellenistic Greek, but a more frequent use is in connection with various words meaning 'abuse'. The common Aramaic use of *ekhal qartzē*, 'eat the pieces of', meaning 'criticize', may have helped here, especially as Paul boasts of being Aramaic-speaking as a boy (the probable meaning of Phil. iii. 5)[1]. However, as *daknete* is used here in close connection with *katesthiete*, 'gulp down', perhaps Paul is still conscious of the original force of the metaphor as referring to conduct more fitting to wild animals than to brothers in Christ. The Old Testament, particularly the Psalter, makes free use of this 'beast' metaphor to describe the attitude of enemies of the people of God (Ps. xxxv. 25, etc.). Almost certainly the reference is to the savage, half-wild, scavenger dogs that still infest many an Eastern city where they were once the only way of disposing of refuse. NEB well translates, 'if you go on fighting one another, tooth and nail', which suggests a cat-fight. Had it not been for the link with *daknete*, and the Old Testament references, we could have translated simply 'destroy', for the

---

[1] For this Aramaic usage, see Jennings, *Syriac New Testament Lexicon*, p. 21.

verb *katesthiō* often has this weakened metaphorical meaning.

analōthēte, *be consumed*, 'be annihilated', is often used of destruction by fire; the basic idea seems to be that nothing at all remains. Paul may be thinking of some ancient story parallel to that of the two Kilkenny cats of Cromwellian times who fought so furiously that not a scrap of fur remained of either.

16. To Paul, the answer to such abuses lies in a way of life which is continually Spirit-controlled; then men will cease to act 'naturally', will cease to 'fulfil themselves'. The use of *peripateite*, 'walk about', in a moral sense is too common to need comment: probably related to this is the use of *hodos*, 'way', to designate the Christian faith (see Acts ix. 2, etc.— though the meaning may be more 'way, sect'). When Paul says *Pneumati* 'by spirit', 'in spirit', it is not always clear whether he is referring directly to the Holy Spirit or not. We may therefore paraphrase as 'a spiritual walk' to keep the ambiguity, although, in the light of what follows, the Holy Spirit is clearly meant.[1]

17. Paul's use of *epithumia*, 'yearning', and the kindred verb, is probably not unconnected with Genesis iv. 7, and traditional Jewish interpretations. Sin's 'desire' is for Cain, but Cain must master it. Even if this is so, however, it is but a verbal similarity, a peg upon which to hang a great theological truth—that 'natural man' does not find the leadings of the Spirit of God to be congenial; indeed, they are utterly repugnant to his own 'natural' inclinations (1 Cor. ii. 14 is a particular instance of this general principle). It is doubtful if the mysterious James iv. 5 is relevant here; but 1 Peter ii. 11 has at least this thought of implacable inner conflict. Paul himself in Romans vii shows that this knowledge of man's inability to do 'what he desires' springs from the inner religious experience of the proud Pharisee. In this sense, *ha ean thelēte*, 'whatever you desire', is to be understood of moral strivings and yearnings, not baser impulses.

[1] See additional note, p. 159, on the meaning of 'pneuma'.

18. This verse seems best taken as a summary of what has gone before rather than as any fresh advance in the argument. There seems to be a continuous force in the present tense of *agesthe*, 'you are being led', as though Paul wished to say 'As long as you are being thus led, then . . .' *Hupo nomon*, in accordance with the principle enunciated above, is to be taken in the general sense of 'law as a principle', rather than the particular 'law of Moses'. Of course, the difference is not great, for the one must include the other. If the Galatians (like all Spirit-led Christians) are not under law as a system, they cannot be under any particular law, whether Jewish or Gentile.

Additional note: the meaning of 'pneuma'

There is a very valuable article under *pneuma* in Arndt-Gingrich, which should be consulted for the various meanings of the word. Like *ruach* in the Old Testament it has travelled far from its original meaning of 'wind, breath', although, especially in John's Gospel, not far enough to make a play on words impossible (cf. Jn. iii. 8). From being the 'breath of life', the immaterial part that alone gives life to the *sarx*, 'flesh', it comes to mean 'self'.[1] Arndt-Gingrich well say 'as the source and seat of insight, feeling, and will, generally as the representative part of the inner life of man'. This is where the ambiguity enters: for *pneumati* (or *en pneumati*) may thus at times mean only 'inwardly', or, at most, 'spiritually'. This is especially so when there is a contrast, explicit or implied, with 'body' or 'flesh'. John iv. 23 is probably an example of this 'generalized' use; while Romans viii. 16, 'the Spirit (of God) bears witness to our very self' (translation following Arndt-Gingrich) shows another ambiguity. Since 'spirit' means 'very self', then it may be used either of man or of God.

When so used of God, the noun 'spirit' usually has the definite article in Greek, and quite often the adjective 'holy' as well. When the word is thus differentiated, it presents no problems.

---

[1] Though this is more often *psuchē* in Greek, corresponding to *nephesh* in Hebrew. See Abbott-Smith on both words and their corresponding Hebrew terms.

This is God's Holy Spirit, sometimes in the New Testament called 'the Spirit of the Lord', or 'the Spirit of Christ', and even 'the Spirit of Jesus' (Acts xvi. 7, RSV). In this sense the Spirit is 'that which differentiates God from everything that is not God. . . . All those who belong to God possess or receive this Spirit and hence have a share in His life. This Spirit also serves to distinguish the Christians from all unbelievers. . . .' (Arndt-Gingrich under *pneuma*).

To Paul, possession of the Spirit is at the same time the possession of the mind of Christ (1 Cor. ii. 16), which alone makes possible the understanding of spiritual truths. Here, however, Paul is more concerned with the fruits of the Spirit in Christlike conduct than the initial revelatory work of the Spirit.

d. The 'natural results' of natural man (v. 19–21)

Paul now moves on to a detailed consideration of the differences produced in a life by the presence of the Spirit. He has already given, in broad outline, the substance of his 'moral argument' which is the main thesis of this section of the letter. Now, in order to point his argument he deals with the contrast between the 'natural' life and the 'spiritual' life in embarrassing detail, no doubt very appropriate to the situation in Galatia. First he gives a list of some of the vices typical of the paganism of his day. There are other equally damning lists in Scripture. Romans i. 29–31 is a classic passage; another is Mark vii. 21, 22, all the more solemn since it comes from the lips of our Lord. Lest Paul be accused of taking an unduly pessimistic view of life, it is well to remember that pagan moralists were, if anything, more severe in their stricture. The one difference was that pagan moralists regarded these things with horror, as contrary to man's true nature; Paul regarded them as the 'natural' results. We can see from Corinthians how Paul had to fight against these vices in all the Gentile churches that he founded. Indeed, it was just because of this floodtide of Gentile immorality that the Judaizers felt the law to be necessary. Jewish churches were not usually so exposed to gross vices of this sort (though Paul's words in Rom. ii. 22 have been thus interpreted by some); their typical sins were

subtler. It is highly likely that Paul's list of vices comes from
a Jewish source.

'What the human nature produces is plain for all to see—
things like unchastity, unnatural vice, sexual excess; idolatry,
magic; hostile feelings, contentiousness, jealousy, temper
tantrums, canvassing for position, dissensions, factions, envy;
alcoholism, wild parties, and all that sort of thing. I tell you
in advance (as I did before) that those who do things like that
will never prove to be heirs of God's kingdom.'

For the exact shade of meaning of each word, the standard
commentaries may be consulted. Burton discusses them in
detail, although his exegesis should be supplemented by more
recent material, such as that in Arndt-Gingrich. The NEB,
with others, tries to divide the vices into groups. First come
three concerned with breaches of sexual law; then two concerned with 'ritual sins', idolatry and sorcery (usually linked
in the Old Testament, as in pagan religions); then eight concerned more with social life; then two dealing with strong
drink. If, as suggested, this comes from some 'Jewish missionary
handbook', used in proselytism of Gentiles, and familiar to
Paul from pre-Christian days, this is all the more likely. The
fact that Paul ends with *and such like* shows us that the list is
by no means exhaustive. Had we the whole gamut, we might
find that it corresponded to the Ten Commandments, or
some other natural division of the law.

It may be, of course, that there is no Jewish prototype for
such a list and that what we have is simply the first sign of
such a Christian 'catalogue', soon to become standard through
the catechetical work of the church. But the similarity of the
description of pagan vices in various parts of the New Testament reads suspiciously as though there had been some
common original. And though the interpretation (and even
the text) of the so-called 'Decree of the Council of Jerusalem'
is doubtful, there is a similar division into sections there (Acts
xv. 29). That this is part of a system of common 'types', no-
one doubts; the only question is as to how far they are original
with Christianity, and how far borrowed from earlier proto-
types, constructed either by Jewish or by Gentile moralists. In

any case, the uniqueness of the Christian understanding both of God and man has, we can be sure, altered the original beyond recognition and made it a new thing, infusing it with a new spirit.

19. It has been sometimes felt that there is an implied contrast between *ta erga, the works*, 'the final products', *of the flesh* and *ho karpos*, the spontaneous *fruit of the Spirit* (verse 22), as though, for all his endeavours, this was the best that natural man could do. The true answer is probably that, while the metaphor of 'fruitbearing' is felt in the case of the Spirit, the metaphor latent in *erga*, works, is so weakened as to be lost in the case of the *flesh*.

The general nature of the vices described will be plain from the paraphrase above (where the definitions follow Arndt-Gingrich in the main), although the lines of demarcation are not always very clear. Indeed, if Paul was using some such kind of traditional 'list' as suggested, it may not always be necessary to look for such distinctions; it may be that the 'piling-up' is for rhetorical effect. *Porneia*, for instance, usually translated 'fornication', seems in point of fact to cover most kinds of 'natural' sexual irregularities—hence the deliberately vague word used in the paraphrase. It is also used in the Old Testament to denote 'idolatry' in the sense of unfaithfulness to God. Since Baal-worship almost invariably involved sexual licence as part of the 'mimetic magic' of its fertility-cult, the gap is not as wide as it appears to us. The other two words probably describe some of the sexual perversions which, as Paul reminds us in Romans i. 26, 27, characterized the pagan world.

20. *Pharmakeia, witchcraft*, RSV 'sorcery', had a special relevance for Asia Minor as can be seen from the story in Acts xix. 19 of the burning of the books containing 'Ephesian Letters', as such magic charms were called in the ancient world. Indeed, the whole atmosphere of the chapter is redolent of magic and spells. The orthodox Jew regarded this sin with peculiar horror, as can be seen from 1 Samuel xv. 23 (where again it is joined with idolatry).

Next come a group of sins which, in view of verse 15, may have had a peculiar relevance to the Galatian situation. Here again the barriers are thin; it will perhaps be sufficient to single out a few of the important and characteristic words. Several will re-occur in other such catalogues of vices elsewhere in the New Testament. *eris*, *variance*, for instance, is clearly something like 'a contentious temper' (so NEB, whose translation of each word in the list is thought-provoking). There seems no point to be made of the fact that the singular is used of this noun while many others are used in the plural when quoted in the list. By the usual Greek rule the plural should mean 'acts of contention'; but Paul uses the plural *erides* in 1 Corinthians i. 11 in substantially the same sense as the singular here.

It is hard to see the distinction between *zēlos* used here and *phthonoi* in the next verse. Both mean 'envy', 'jealousy'. Perhaps Paul's use of *zēlos* goes back to the use of the cognate verb in iv. 17, 18, referring to the activity of the Judaizers. Clearly, the whole sense of *zēlos* is bad here, whatever we may decide about the usage in the earlier passage.

eritheiai is well translated by NEB as 'selfish ambitions', although it more properly denotes the unfair 'canvassing for office' which is prompted by such ambitions (see Arndt-Gingrich). Any linguistic connection with *eris* is very doubtful. Distinct from it is *haireseis*, which, although giving English 'heresies', probably means 'factions', as in 1 Corinthians xi. 19. The NEB translation, 'party intrigues', may be a little too strong, but conveys the right idea.

21. *methai* (lit. 'drunkennesses') and *kōmoi*, 'carousings', probably both refer primarily to the drunken orgies at festivals of the pagan gods, and secondarily to the general insobriety of pagan life. Alcoholism and wild beach-parties of teenagers might be our nearest modern equivalents. We can see from 1 Corinthians xi. 21 how easily such abuses could creep even into the Lord's Supper in Gentile churches.

When Paul says 'as I warned you before' (RSV, NEB), we are faced with the same problem as in i. 9 where the perfect tense of the same verb (*proeirēkamen*, 'we said beforehand') occurred. When had Paul delivered this warning? In this instance it is difficult to find an earlier context in the same letter to justify the use; nor can we assume a 'lost' earlier letter to the Galatians as we might perhaps in the case of other churches such as Corinth. The only logical conclusion, therefore, is that Paul in his initial evangelizing was far from restricting himself to the 'simple gospel' as sometimes we erroneously suppose. He must also have given much strong moral teaching. This in itself gives the lie to the Jewish charge that he taught freedom from all moral restraints (Rom. iii. 8). Admittedly, if the letter is regarded as being addressed to South Galatia, the narrative in Acts is very brief (chapters xiii and xiv); but on the return journey some such moral instruction is suggested.

Although Paul has said that we cannot by 'doing' *inherit the kingdom of God*, that is win entrance to it (Christ is the door, and such a door opens only to faith), yet he strongly asserts here that by 'doing' we can bar ourselves from that kingdom. This is not the paradox that it seems at first sight. Paul's whole point is that *they which do such things* thereby show themselves to be without the transforming gift of faith. The reaction in Romans vi. 1 to the question 'Are we to continue in sin, that grace may abound?' is exactly the same: 'God forbid.' To all these things the Christian has died already; therefore he shows the reality of the 'faith that justifies', and the reality of the new 'life in Christ' that is within him, by a clear break with all these 'works of darkness', familiar though they may have been to him in the past. It comes as a shock to respectable suburban Christianity when Paul, in 1 Corinthians vi. 11, after a list of loathsome vices, says calmly 'Some of you were once like that'—although he does hasten to reassure the Corinthians of their new standing in Christ.

The reference to 'will never prove to be heirs', *ou klēronomēsousin*, goes back to the discussion about Abraham and his 'offspring' in chapter iii. Paul has shown in iv. 7 that, if we are sons, then, by the same token, we are heirs, *klēronomoi* ('joint-heirs with Christ', as Rom. viii. 17 has it). But chapter iv had ended with the stern warning that the children of the slave-wife, themselves slaves, cannot share in God's promised wealth of glory; indeed, they are specifically excluded. So here. Those who are 'slaves' to such passions show themselves to be no true-born sons of the king; such can never inherit the kingdom.

Additional note: the 'kingdom of God'

Paul's use of *basileian Theou*, 'God's kingdom', is very interesting. The concept of the 'kingdom of God' is dominant in the Gospels, especially perhaps in Matthew, who writes in a thoroughly Jewish milieu and as the heir to a long Old Testament tradition. But it is just as discernible in the other Synoptics; and even John, in typical Johannine fashion, introduces the concept, especially in his closing chapters (e.g. Jn. xviii. 33–38). The image is freely used in the book of Acts. Indeed, Acts xiv. 22 (if we are supporters of the South Galatian theory) shows us Paul teaching to these very Galatians 'that through many tribulations we must enter the kingdom of God' (RSV). Paul himself uses the analogy more often than might be supposed; Romans xiv. 17 and 1 Corinthians iv. 20 are two random instances. For 'inheriting the kingdom' (a thoroughly Jewish concept, derived from the Old Testament) see 1 Corinthians vi. 9 and Ephesians v. 5. Paul therefore seems to have employed the picture consistently through his ministry, whether early or late, Jewish or Gentile. It is however true to say that, although present in Pauline theology, it is not a dominant concept. Paul prefers to speak in terms of 'gospel' and 'church', for instance, rather than 'kingdom'. This is not of course to identify these completely, but merely to say that all three belong to the same realm of ideas, in the sense that they describe the relation of God with man. *basileia* itself would actually be better translated as 'rule of God' (or, with Moffatt, 'realm of God') rather than 'kingdom', which to English ears suggests a spatial and temporal location.[1]

[1] For 'kingdom' as an eschatological concept, see, as well as the standard commentators on Matthew, Arndt-Gingrich, with literature quoted under the word.

e. The harvest of the Spirit (v. 22–26)

Now comes a corresponding list of spiritual qualities. Although such a roll-call exists in other parts of the New Testament (as in 2 Peter i. 5–7) there is no such close similarity as in the classification of the vices (the Petrine list, for instance, is in the reverse order, with *agapē*, 'love', as the climax). This suggests that no Hebrew prototype existed, but that lists of the spiritual qualities are a Christian creation. It seems obvious that, while Judaism and Christianity might well agree on what were vices, their concept of virtues might be very different.

'But, by contrast, the harvest that the Spirit brings is love, joy, tranquillity, forbearance with others, kindness, generosity, reliability, humility, self-control in the realm of sex. There is no law against men who act like this. For those who belong to Christ Jesus have put their "flesh" to death, along with all its passionate desires. Now, as surely as we are living by the rule of the Spirit, let us walk by the rule of the Spirit. Let us, for instance, not be boastful, challenging and envying one another's position.'

For the reasons leading to the choice of terms in this translation, see Arndt-Gingrich under the various words. Again, the difficulty is to know where to draw the line of demarcation between one virtue and another. In most cases the 'areas of meaning' overlap considerably. Also, without giving a very loose paraphrase, it is not easy to cover all the shades of meaning; so an attempt has been made to select that one word which seems most appropriate to this context and to the presumed position in Galatia.

22. The first three aspects of the Spirit's harvest need little comment; *chara, joy,* and *eirēnē, peace,* are probably suggested by the typically Jewish-Christian greeting of 'grace and peace', '*charis kai eirēnē*' of i. 3. To the Christian joy is something independent of outward circumstances; other instances of its junction with the Holy Spirit are 1 Thessalonians i. 6 and Romans xiv. 17. *Agapē* has been already considered; it is put first as embracing all the others if rightly understood. Whether we are justified in bracketing these three as a triad apart from the other virtues is uncertain. The list certainly does not fall into sections as readily as that of the vices did. (See 1 Cor. xiii. 13 for another triad.)

The use of *karpos*, *fruit*, as mentioned above, suggests that all these spiritual qualities, and many more, are the spontaneous product of the presence of the Spirit of Christ within the heart of the Christian. The metaphor is a very old one with its roots deep in the soil of the Old Testament. Perhaps we might add that it is a metaphor natural to an agricultural people like Israel. While *karpos* means any kind of fruit, it is most frequently employed of the product of the fruit-tree or vine. John uses it in the latter sense in chapter xv of his Gospel. It was a principle enunciated by the Lord Himself that a tree could be recognized by the fruit that it bore (Mt. vii. 16); so, by the presence of these 'fruits', the presence of the Spirit is proved.

makrothumia, *longsuffering*, is translated by RSV and NEB as 'patience'; perhaps 'tolerance' would give the idea better in modern English. It is the quality of putting up with other people, even when patience is sorely tried. One wonders why Paul put it in such a lofty place in his list. Perhaps it was because in Galatia neither 'party' displayed much of this virtue. *chrēstotēs* has been translated in the paraphrase above as 'kindness' (so also RSV, NEB). It also has the connotations of 'goodness' and 'generosity' (see Arndt-Gingrich), but these are covered by other words in the list before us. The common slave-name *Chrēstos* comes from this root, so that it suggests some quality that was looked for in the ideal servant. It is highly probable that the first-century pagans confused this familiar name with the unfamiliar *Christos* (both being pronounced the same by that time) and that, in their view, the new nickname *Christianoi* was really *Chrēstianoi* (Acts xi. 26). One is tempted to speculate whether the wits of Antioch intended the pun when they called this 'reformed sect' of Judaism 'the goody-goodies'. *agathōsunē* has probably more of its colloquial meaning of 'generosity' than its original meaning of *goodness* although both are possible: *prautēs* (verse 23) would then be something like 'humility' (AV, *meekness*), or 'gentleness' (SO RSV, NEB).

These qualities are indisputably manward in their aspect, and most, if not all, are directly relevant to the postulated state of party strife in the Galatian churches, whether two-sided or three-sided. It is interesting that most of them are qualities to be displayed by the victor to the vanquished. That in itself suggests that Paul fears over-violent dealing with the Judaizers by the victorious 'orthodox party' in the church. The apostle's exhortation in vi. 1 bears this out. Once Paul has vanquished an opponent in argument, he ceases, for Paul, to be an opponent and becomes instead an erring brother in need of pastoral care. But he knows human nature too well to expect that the Galatian reaction will be the same. Indeed, the more tempted the Galatians had been to succumb to the attack of the Judaizers, the more likely they would be to lead the 'heresy-hunt' now. Human nature is like that; we do not need a psychologist to show us this truth.

Of the two remaining qualities, *pistis*, usually translated *faith*, would seem to be directed to God, not to man. However, it can equally well be translated as in RSV 'faithfulness' (NEB 'fidelity'; we have seen this meaning inherent in the Habakkuk quotation of iii. 11). If this is the correct rendering, it could apply to the Christian's attitude manwards as well as God-wards. It could then refer to the Galatian's lack of faith towards Paul of which he is complaining in iv. 12–20.

23. The last quality, *enkrateia*, 'self-control', is neither God-ward nor manward, but more properly selfward. It is usually employed to describe self-control in sexual matters; if that is its meaning here, then it refers back to the grosser vices of v. 19. It is not only that Paul wants to heighten the contrast by two corresponding 'panels' of virtues and vices; if there was a 'libertine' party at Galatia, boasting of their 'freedom', then they sorely needed this gift. 1 Corinthians vii. 7 seems to describe this power of continence as a *charisma*, a special 'spiritual gift', while 1 Thessalonians iv. 4–8 likewise connects right Christian behaviour in these matters with the Holy

Spirit. *tōn toioutōn* could be translated, with NEB, as 'such things as these', and the sense would be excellent. No law forbids qualities like these; and as the law is seen in this context as a set of negative precepts, this means that such virtues are in fact the 'keeping', or 'fulfilling', of the law. But, in view of the personal nature of the reference in verse 21 where *hoi toiauta prassontes* clearly means 'those who habitually behave thus', it is better to translate as 'such men' here. The phrase will then become 'The law was never meant for (or "never directed against") men like this'. In either case, the main sense is the same.

24. Paul now gives the reason both for the production of this rich spiritual harvest and for the freedom of the Christian from the law. He is one who has already 'put his old self to death', *tēn sarka estaurōsan*. As before, 'original nature' is perhaps a strong enough equivalent for *sarx*; to say 'lower nature' (with NEB) is to suggest that man is really capable of higher things, and this Paul will not allow. The point of *estaurōsan*, *crucified*, is to link this total change in attitude, and therefore conduct, with the death of Christ. It is another way of expressing Galatians ii. 20, 'I have been crucified with Christ.' There were many other words that Paul could have used, like 'die' or 'abolish', which would have conveyed his general meaning, but not this nuance. Romans vi. 6 has almost exactly the same thought, except that Paul there uses *palaios anthrōpos*, 'old man', instead of *sarx*, 'flesh'.

pathēmasin, 'passions', and *epithumiais*, 'longings', are to be taken closely together; so to translate 'passionate longings' is not misleading. Hebrew was chary in the use of adjectives, as were many ancient languages. Often two nouns, juxtaposed, would serve the purpose as well. Either through the Greek translation of the Old Testament, or through the persistence of old speech-habits in those whose mother-tongue was not Greek, the same linguistic tendency appears in the New Testament, though in reduced form. Like *pathos*, the word *pathēma* has a twofold meaning, either (in a good sense) 'suffering', or (in a bad sense) 'passion', usually of a sexual nature. The *epithumia*, 'longing' (of the flesh) is taken from verse 17 above, where the cognate verb occurs.

25. The use of *Pneumati*, 'by Spirit', or 'in Spirit', has the same ambiguity as before, in that it may have a general or a specific reference. If general, we must translate 'spiritually'; if specific, we may follow the NEB: 'If the Spirit is the source of our life, let the Spirit also direct our course.' Again, the *ei*, *if*, does not express any sense of contingency or doubt; rather it means 'since . . .'

26. At first sight this verse might look as though its function was simply to sum up the fruits of the Spirit already mentioned. But it is more than that, for it is leading to a particular application. The hazarded guess is that it is a direct application to the Galatian situation. This 'spiritual' way of life, says Paul, utterly forbids all forms of ambitious rivalry and envy. This sounds suspiciously as though there were party strife in the church of the type most familiar to us from Corinth. It may be, of course, that we need not seek for a particular application; Paul was so well acquainted with human nature, from the pastoral care of so many churches, that he knew this was a danger everywhere, and therefore cautioned them against it. *kenodoxoi* means either 'conceited' or 'boastful'. Perhaps the danger was that those who had not fallen to the Judaizing error were now boasting of their superior spiritual strength, while those who had given way were *phthonountes*, 'envious', 'jealous'. Alternatively, the trouble may be a simple struggle for power within the church; we may be wrong in seeking for deeper motives.

f. How to deal with the offender (vi. 1–6)

If the interpretation suggested above is correct, if only along general lines, then Paul is now turning to the specific question of how the church should deal with the repentant Judaizer, actual or imagined. The use of the singular may again refer either to some known individual ringleader (probably in this case inside the church), or may be used, with studied indifference, to describe the group. If he was one who claimed leadership and some special position for himself, then the application of verse 4 would be obvious; while, if he had actually been a 'teaching elder' in the church, then verse 6 would be full of local relevance. The great danger, however, in all New Testament Epistles is that of reading in too much, particularly when we are almost without knowledge as to the actual local background. But if we do not adopt some such system of interpretation with the coherence that it gives to the whole passage, then we must assume that these closing sections are a mere theological 'portmanteau', into which Paul bundles a sequence of unrelated injunctions. This is always possible; some of the remarks at the end of his major Epistles read suspiciously like postscripts. But it does not seem likely here.

Further, we have a very close parallel from the Corinthian correspondence where Pauls speaks specifically of the duty of 'winning back' the erring brother (2 Cor. ii. 5–11). Certainly the existence of party strife in Galatia is a close parallel to the situation at Corinth; but how far we can justifiably press the analogy is uncertain.

'Fellow-Christians, even if a man be caught doing something wrong, you who are "the spiritual party" must set him to rights in a gentle, humble way. Watch yourself; you may be tested too. Carry heavy loads for one another; that is how you will observe Christ's law to the full. If anyone thinks himself to be quite a Somebody (when he is really a Nobody), all he is doing is to hoodwink himself. Let each man carefully weigh up what he has actually achieved, and then he can have pride in his own work, not in someone else's. For each man will have to shoulder his own pack. But the one who is being taught Christian doctrine ought to share with his teacher all the good things that he has.'

1. *prolēmphthē* can mean either 'to be caught (doing something wrong)' (so NEB mg.), or, in a more vivid sense 'should (do something wrong) on a sudden impulse' (NEB text). The latter is more vivid, but does not suit the context so well especially if there is a reference to Judaizing. That could hardly be described as 'a sudden impulse'—unless willingness to accept circumcision is so described. The subject is the suitably vague *anthrōpos, a man,* 'anybody'. Whether we regard the vagueness as deliberate or no will depend upon our interpretation of the whole situation. If this is the local ringleader in the Judaizing movement, then we must agree that the *tis,* 'somebody, anybody', of verse 3 is equally specific and pointed in its reference.

Who are the *pneumatikoi,* the 'spiritually-minded'? Paul may use the word at its face value as meaning, 'You who are walking by the rule of the Spirit.' In that case it would be a straightforward appeal to the unfallen to assist the fallen. But in view of the later use of the word *pneumatikos* as the self-chosen title of those who boasted themselves of a superior spiritual position, some have suspected a deeper meaning here. It is as though Paul were saying: 'You claim a superior spirituality? Prove it, then, by acting spiritually in this case.' The later Gnostic associations of the word (as meaning those who are 'libertines' because they are free from all restraints save those of the direct leadings of the Spirit) are probably irrelevant here. It is quite likely that one of the parties in Galatia used this as a title. 1 Corinthians iii. 1, however, uses the word in a good sense as opposed to *sarkinoi,* 'earthy-minded Christians', and *nēpioi,* 'immature Christians'. So, even if it was a party-name in Galatia, there is no need to associate it as yet with the 'immoral' group to whom some of Paul's other injunctions are directed. *katartizete* is either 'restore to its former condition' or 'complete'. The first of these meanings is highly suitable to describe the restoration of a Christian who has 'lapsed', whether by Judaizing or in any other way. The Gospels use the word of 'mending nets' (Mt. iv. 21). In *skopōn,* 'keeping an eye on', Pauls changes very vividly from the plural to the singular. It is as though he changes from the collective duty of the church to the duty of each individual member. *skopōn,* while basically meaning 'look', has the colloquial sense of 'look out for', exactly like the corresponding verb in English.

2. This verse introduces yet another use of *bastazete, bear,* 'shoulder'. In v. 10 it was used of the Arch-Judaizer; he will yet 'bear' or 'endure' the heavy judgment of God. Here it is again used of shouldering a heavy burden; but this time the burden is a good one, a load of responsibility and care (unless with NEB we translate 'help one another to carry these heavy loads', where the thought is the burden of shame of the guilty sinner). In verse 5, when used with *phortion*, the meaning is lighter still, and seems to be more in the nature of 'shoulder a pack', as a porter or pedlar might do. The last use of the word in the Epistle will be the most significant of all: in vi. 17, Paul will say *bastazō*, 'I carry about in my body the marks of the Lord Jesus'. The meaning of the *stigmata*, 'marks', will be considered below; but this use of the verb makes us wonder if Paul does not here remember how Jesus in John xix. 17 is pictured as *bastazōn*, 'shouldering', His cross on the way to Golgotha.

The phrase *ton nomon tou Christou, the law of Christ*, is arresting. This is the closest that Paul ever comes to setting 'Christ's law' over against 'Moses' law'; and had it not been in the context of the peculiar problem of the Galatians, he might not have put it so bluntly. Yet, after all, Paul is doing no more here than the Lord does in John xiii. 34, with His 'A new commandment I give to you'. Yet nevertheless in the context of *anaplērōsate*, 'you will fulfil', the clause takes on deeper meaning. The Galatians and their teachers had been eager to keep the law of Moses; but here was a higher way by which they might keep the law of Christ. The early fathers used this term extensively. The roots seem to lie in this Pauline passage, for Romans iii. 27 is using *nomos* in the more general sense of 'principle'.

3. The phrase *dokei tis einai*, meaning either 'thinks he is a somebody' or 'seems to be a somebody', reminds us of the threefold use of *hoi dokountes* ('the powers that be') in chapter ii, describing the Jerusalem 'apostles'. Here the reference is probably entirely general; *dokei*, 'seems', is violently contrasted with *ōn*, 'actually being', and *tis*, 'a somebody', with *mēden*, 'a nobody', 'a nothing'. A more crushing assessment could hardly be made of one who, at best, can have been nothing more than a large frog in a small pool. But Paul is probably thinking more of the man's poor spiritual state than of his unimportance.

This is the sole use of the word *phrenapata*, 'deceives, hoodwinks', in the New Testament (although other words for 'deceive' abound). The cognate noun *phrenapatēs*, 'deceiver', occurs however in Titus i. 10. Perhaps Paul's choice of the word here is governed by the fact that such a man has been 'too clever by half', as the colloquial tongue has it. He has succeeded in taking himself in, although he has deceived nobody else. (*phrēn* by itself means 'mind', 'intellect', and *apataō* means 'deceive'.)

4. What Paul means by saying *let every man prove* (or 'scrutinize') *his own work* (*ergon*, 'achievement') is not wholly clear. It depends upon whether we should translate strictly with this context in view, or whether we may use the presumably similar situations described in other Pauline letters as analogy. NEB seems to translate in the first way with 'Each man should examine his own conduct for himself; then he can measure his achievement by comparing himself with himself and not with anyone else'. The second half of this translation perhaps deals a little freely with *kauchēma*, 'boasting', 'object of boasting'; but the first half is quite possible. In Paul's writings, however, *dokimazō*, 'test', and its cognates are often used of the scrutiny of God applied to the work of the Christian evangelist or teacher; and this seems likely here too, especially in view of the general background of the Epistle. Paul may be thinking both of the 'work' of the Judaizing teachers (which will not endure the divine scrutiny) and his own (which will).[1] This would have the advantage of introducing as well the reason for *kauchēma*, 'boasting'. The Galatians have been boasting in the 'work' of the Judaizers, shoddy though it was.

5. Paul uses *kauchēma*, 'boasting', very frequently of 'the object of boasting' (e.g. 2 Cor. i. 14, Phil. ii. 16). For Paul,

---

[1] 1 Corinthians iii. 12–15 is the classic passage for the judgment on the 'worker'.

his converts are his typical *kauchēma* in the day of Christ (as in the passage from Philippians quoted). Paul may mean that the Judaizers do well not to 'count scalps', but to see where they stand themselves, in view of the coming judgment. For, on that day, each of us must be answerable for ourselves (J. B. Phillips, 'every man must "shoulder his own pack" '). There is thus no contradiction between this declaration of individual responsibility before the Lord and the general injunction given in verse 2, to bear one another's burdens (where the word is *barē*, 'heavy loads').

6. It is, as often, difficult to decide whether this is the final verse of this section or the opening clause of the next. As usual, it will be best to take it as a 'bridge verse', whichever group it is considered as falling under. The one who is *katēchoumenos ton logon* is clearly 'under Christian instruction': thus it is legitimate to gloss the plain word *logon* as 'in the faith' (so NEB). Whether this implies as yet any highly developed catechetical system in the infant Church is extremely uncertain.[1] Therefore we may translate in a general sense and interpret the verse as describing the relation between 'teacher' and 'taught', without assuming too set a pattern. The reference may be to a 'teaching elder' (see 1 Tim. v. 17 for the existence of such men). If the one who led the Galatians astray had been one in authority in the church, then this injunction would have new meaning; but it may of course be quite general in application. When Paul says *koinōneitō*, 'let him have fellowship', it is a Christian euphemism for 'let him make a financial contribution'. To Paul, this phraseology is more than an exhibition of oriental courtesy; such Christian giving is the only fit expression of that *koinōnia*, 'sharing', 'fellowship', which marks the common life in Christ.[2]

[1] See Arndt-Gingrich under *homologia*, 'confession', as well as under *katēcheō*. Hunter, Carrington, and Cullmann are great names; but while in the days of the Apostolic Fathers we are probably justified in seeing such a technical use, it is unlikely as early as the pages of the New Testament.

[2] One of his chief concerns among the Gentile churches was to encourage them to make such contributions to the church at Jerusalem. Romans xv. 27 exemplifies this principle.

g. Sowing and reaping (vi. 7-10)

Paul now returns to the idea suggested by v. 22, with its metaphor of 'fruit of the Spirit'. While *karpos*, as noted there, is more commonly used of 'fruits', it can also be used of 'grain', and the metaphor here is that of grain harvested. This again is a very old biblical simile, used frequently by the Lord both in parable and incidental allusion, though principally with reference to the evangelizing tasks of His disciples (as for instance in Mt. ix. 37). It is worth considering whether the metaphor may not have been re-suggested to Paul's mind by the treatment of Christian giving in the verse immediately before. Paul often sees 'charity' in terms of 'sowing'; 2 Corinthians ix. 6 is a good example which will be noted below.

'Make no mistake about this: you cannot turn up your nose at God. A man will harvest exactly what he sows. I mean that the man who sows as his own nature bids him will reap a harvest of corruption from that nature; but the man who sows as the Spirit bids him will reap from that Spirit a harvest of life eternal. So let us never lose heart and give up doing what is good. When the right time comes we will reap a harvest —if only we do not give up now, through weariness. Well then, whenever we have opportunity, let us work for the common good, especially for the good of those who are our blood-relatives in the Christian faith.'

7. *planasthe*, 'be led astray', is one of the commonest words in the New Testament for *deceived*. It does suggest, in its passive form here, that the Galatians have been 'led astray' in this matter by some from outside. The two clauses are sharply juxtaposed in what is really paratax, not syntax: 'Do not be led astray—you cannot mock God.' The NEB translates *muktērizetai* as 'fooled'. Its rendering 'God is not to be fooled' gives the general meaning, but if we can keep 'turn up the nose at', the etymology will be reproduced in English.[1]

This verse, both in view of its general rhythmic nature and in view of its constant recurrence in roughly similar forms, probably represents a folk-saying found in many languages.

[1] See Arndt-Gingrich for further remarks on this interesting word.

2 Corinthians ix. 6 is another rhythmical presentation of the theme.

8. When Paul says of a man, 'If he sows seed in the field of his lower nature, he will reap from it a harvest of corruption' (NEB), he means more than that we must reap the wild oats which we sow. To him, *phthora, corruption*, is not only (or even primarily) moral decay; it is that physical decay which inevitably awaits this mortal frame (whether described as *sōma*, 'body', or *sarx*, 'flesh'), and fitly reminds us of the fallen state of our human nature (1 Cor. xv. 42). Indeed, since to the Hebrew mind death was so closely connected with sin, it is doubtful if he would have made the distinction between 'moral' and 'physical' corruption which we find so congenial to our thought-patterns. The physical death and decay are but the consequences of the spiritual and moral death and decay that are present already. That is why for the Christian the doctrine of resurrection is so closely connected with that of the new birth. Once he is removed from the realm of sin he is also removed from the realm of death, sin's grim ally. So here the opposite of *phthora, corruption*, is *zōēn aiōnion, life everlasting*, one of the many biblical expressions for the present enjoyment of that life of God which is salvation. This *zōē* occupies a central thought in the presentation of the gospel by John; the present passage, among others, shows that this concept was also part of the common substratum of Christianity. To see 'salvation' in terms of 'life' is as old as the Old Testament (e.g. Ps. xvi. 11, chosen at random); but in the New Testament the concept takes on a new richness. There is an excellent article in Arndt-Gingrich under the word, with a full bibliography.

9, 10. While Paul never wearies of telling men that they cannot win God's favour by good deeds, he equally never wearies of telling them of their duty to *do good*. Twice in this short passage the idea recurs, with *to kalon poiountes*, 'doing what is good', in verse 9, and *ergazōmetha to agathon*, probably 'let us do what is good', in verse 10. It is doubtful if there is any distinction intended between the two words for 'do' (*poiein*, *ergazesthai*) and 'good' (*kalos, agathos*); the probable reason for the choice is a desire for variety. NEB may be right, however, in translating the last phrase as 'Let us work for the good of all'. Romans viii. 28 would then be a roughly similar usage. But this is only a minor point of interpretation not affecting the main issue of the plain duty of a Christian man.

There is only one danger that faces the 'spiritual farmer'; there is only one thing that can hinder this harvest. It is doubly expressed here as *mē enkakōmen* and *mē ekluomenoi*. *enkakeō* is properly 'to lose heart', 'to despair'. Outside the Bible it is used of a woman's fears in child-birth. 'Giving in to evil' or 'giving in to difficulty' seems to be the original idea; but it soon takes on the weaker sense 'to grow weary'. In Luke xviii. 1 the Lord warns us that this is the danger which may stop our persistent prayer. 2 Corinthians iv. 1 shows that it is a temptation firmly put from him by the apostle to the Gentiles. *ekluomai*, with a very different etymology, comes to signify almost the same thing. It seems to mean originally the opposite of 'gird up'. As the Jew 'tightened his belt' to do work, so when he 'loosened his belt' it meant he had abandoned effort. This sprang, of course, from the flowing nature of the garment; if not 'girded up' it would only impede the worker. Arndt-Gingrich suggest 'become slack', which seems to preserve the metaphor in English; but in the medical writers, when used in the passive, it means something like 'become limp', 'grow weary'. As describing a disheartened farmer the picture is very graphic; as describing the disheartened Galatians who have found so much previous 'effort' vain it is equally striking.

Another word upon which Paul plays in this context is *kairos*, 'time'. It has often been remarked that *chronos* is 'time in the abstract', while *kairos* means 'the right time' for anything, and thus *opportunity*. That is certainly true of both instances here. We cannot hope to reap our harvest before God's time comes (but see Jn. iv. 35 for the present harvest). Nevertheless, now is God's time to do good to all, especially to our fellow Christians; we have a present opportunity to do good and we reject it at our peril.

The words used for 'fellow Christians', *oikeious tēs pisteōs*, really mean 'those who have become related to us by a common faith'. This is a highly compressed way of saying that they, like us, have been born into God's family by their faith in Christ. Therefore, says Paul, they have a peculiar claim upon us. The word is thus virtually equivalent to *tous hagious*, 'the saints', or *tous adelphous*, 'the brothers', used elsewhere. In that case, since *do good* almost certainly means 'give alms', there may be an inner meaning. Paul may be trying to collect for the Jerusalem poor.

Although this may seem at first to be a 'long shot', there is much in the context to make it possible, if not actually to commend it. ii. 10 has already referred to Paul's habit of taking a collection to aid the 'poor saints'; if the atmosphere in Galatia is still too stormy to mention the matter directly, that need not surprise us. In that case, 'teacher' and 'taught' of verse 6 could be Jewish Christian and Gentile Christian respectively: and the parallel with Romans xv. 27 becomes closer. The 'sowing' and 'reaping' of verse 7 would then apply primarily to almsgiving, although Paul cannot resist giving the saying a moral 'twist' as he quotes it. This again comes closer to 2 Corinthians ix. 6. It is obvious that the most faithful of Gentile Christians might lose heart in doing such good works when he saw how the Judaizers of the Jerusalem church rewarded him. Was Paul speaking as much to his own heart as to theirs? Were there times when even he almost lost heart and wondered if he could ever win over these stubborn, narrow-minded men by these deeds of love? We cannot say. All we know is that neither Paul nor the Gentile churches did in point of fact flag in this unselfish, loving service.

h. The autographed conclusion (vi. 11-18)

The letter is over now. Paul takes the pen from his amanuensis (assuming that he has not written the whole) to write 'The Grace' in his own handwriting—his usual practice to assure them of the genuineness of the letter. But as he looks at the big sprawling letters, he muses whimsically that they certainly make no fine outward show, and this becomes to him a parable of the whole of his life. As far as he is now concerned there is nothing 'fine' in life but the cross of Christ; and he brushes the last vestiges of the quarrel from him in the knowledge of his own close relation to the crucified One. On that note of peace the battle-scarred veteran ends the tortured letter.

'See how big letters I am using now that I am writing myself. It is those who want to "show off" and put a fine face on things who are trying to force you to get yourselves circumcised; it is only to avoid being persecuted for the sake of the cross of the Messiah. For not even those who do accept circumcision as a rite keep the law—and now they want you to get your-selves circumcised so that they may have something to boast about in outward terms. May I never boast in anything at all, except in the cross of our Lord Jesus Christ, by which[1] the world has been crucified as far as I am concerned, and I as far as the world is concerned. To be circumcised means nothing; to be uncircumcised means nothing; the only thing that matters is to be created anew. Peace and mercy be upon all those who make this their rule of thumb—and upon God's Israel. In future let no-one bother me. I carry round with me Christ's marks, stamped on my body. The grace of our Lord Jesus Christ be with your spirit, my fellow Christians. Amen.'

11. *pēlikois grammasin* probably refers to the sprawling untidy letters of one not a scribe by trade, and who was, perhaps, more used to writing in Semitic characters than Greek. If the rest of the letter were 'professionally' written then the contrast would be immediate. Most editors take *pēlikois* quite literally as meaning 'how big'; for other suggestions, see Arndt-Gingrich under the word. Those who see Paul's recurrent illness as ophthalmia or something similar will point to the large letters often written by the half-blind. But half-literate people also normally use large lettering, and no man has yet accused Paul of falling under that category.

12. *euprosōpēsai* (occurring only here in the New Testament) means 'make a good showing'. For *en sarki*, to be taken closely

---

[1] It is possible that in verse 14 we should follow NEB margin with 'by whom' rather than NEB text with 'by which'. The Greek is ambiguous.

with it, Arndt-Gingrich suggest 'before men'. The Gentile would smile at the idea that circumcision could be considered *a fair shew* by the Jew; to him it was a disfiguring custom, like savage tattooing. But Paul's point was that the Jews wanted 'ecclesiastical statistics'; so many circumcisions in a given year was certainly something to boast about. It is easy to smile at them. But 'baptismal statistics' in mission areas can at times be just as dangerous if seen as a goal. Besides, the Jews honestly believed circumcision achieved something; to them it was the gateway to the covenant. Paul saw equally clearly that to accept circumcision meant that the whole 'sting' of the cross was gone. No longer was there an 'either/or': there was only a 'both/and'. An eirenic age like our own needs to remember Paul's explosion, and the theology that lay behind it.

13. *hoi peritemnomenoi*, 'those becoming circumcised' (or perhaps 'the circumcisers') is best taken here of the Jews whose habitual practice it is rather than of the Gentiles who are now tempted to take the step. Admittedly this is a different sense from that of v. 3, but the different context seems to warrant it. In that case, it is used in the sense of the more usual *peritomē*, 'circumcision', used as synonym for the Jewish nation. This meaning would suit Paul's rebuke. The Jews themselves have failed to keep the law; why try to involve Gentiles in the same failure by persuading them to accept the rite that binds to the law?

Once again comes a play on words, this time on the verb *kauchasthai*, 'to boast'. The noun Paul has used already in his warning of verse 4. Now he says that the only possible reason for the Jewish proselytizing zeal (for which see Mt. xxiii. 15) must be a desire to 'boast' in their outward condition of circumcision; for he has already shown that this outward rite cannot work any inward change in them.

14, 15. As a counter to all this one would expect Paul to 'boast' in uncircumcision. But he cannot do that for he, just as much as they, is a circumcised Jew. Instead, he dismisses the whole subject by saying that neither of the outward states is important, or even relevant. He could neither boast of being circumcised if he were a Jew, nor of being uncircumcised if he were a Gentile. The one thing that he can 'boast' about is the cross of Jesus Christ which has made all such distinctions meaningless; for it completely breaks the connection with the old 'outward world' and gives both Jew and Gentile a new perspective. The only thing that matters now is that Jew and Gentile alike are 'newly-created men' in Christ, a new sort of men, with a new way of looking at everything. The theology of this passage is finely expressed in 2 Corinthians v. 16, 17, again in the direct context of the cross of Christ. The ultimate condemnation of the Judaizers is that they are still looking at things 'from a human point of view' (2 Cor. v. 16, RSV); but if that be truly so they cannot yet be 'in Christ'.

The *kainē ktisis*, 'new creation', is a favourite thought of Paul's. Just as Genesis showed a creation marred and spoiled by sin, so surely in prophet and apocalyptist arose the picture of a new universe, a new *ktisis* of God (e.g. Is. lxv. 17 taken up by Rev. xxi. 1) in which God's active work as Creator is stressed. Here, as in the 2 Corinthians passage, the word is probably to be translated *creature* rather than 'creation' (as in AV); that is to say, the reference is to the regenerating work of God in the individual soul rather than to the total result thus secured.[1]

16. When Paul says *tō kanoni toutō stoichēsousin*, 'live their lives according to this principle', he is referring to the spiritual experience and resultant attitude described immediately above. Such men truly have 'the mind of Christ' (1 Cor. ii. 16); they have God's way of looking at things, not man's way (1 Sa. xvi. 7). Paul has already used *stoicheō* of the Christian 'walk' in v. 25 where it was in connection with *pneuma*, 'the Spirit'. With the dative it usually has a more metaphorical sense, 'hold to', 'agree with', 'follow with' (see Arndt-Gingrich). Acts xxi. 24 is significant; James uses it there, with *phulassōn ton nomon*, 'keeping the law', to describe Paul's habitual atti-

---

[1] Romans viii. 39 and Hebrews iv. 13 clearly have this sense. Romans viii. 19–22, on the other hand, with its reference to the coming 'cosmic redemption' probably refers to the whole animate and inanimate creation below man. See Arndt-Gingrich and Cullmann as quoted there.

tude and behaviour. But here Paul shows that the Christian governs his life by a far higher principle (*kanoni*; the word has not yet the technical meaning of 'rule of faith', acquired in the later church). The old, generally accepted text of Philippians iii. 16 has *kanoni* in the same sense; but the better witnesses to the text omit it as a 'gloss' from this passage.

The second half of verse 16 poses a question of interpretation which hangs on the exact meaning of the introductory *kai*. Does the word mean 'and', 'in addition to', or 'even', 'that is to say'? A strong case can be made for both views. If the word is to be translated 'and', then Paul's final prayer is directed towards those Gentiles who realize the unimportance of their physical state, and to Jews who likewise realize the unimportance of circumcision. By so doing, they prove themselves to be the true Israel, God's Israel, the 'righteous remnant'. To them circumcision is a matter of the heart, not of the body (Rom. ii. 29). This would link closely with the two groups described in verse 15 as *peritomē* and *akrobustia* ('circumcision' and 'uncircumcision'—the latter probably being a Jewish play on words; see Arndt-Gingrich). It would also be a fitting olive-branch stretched out to 'orthodox' Jewish Christianity, lest they should think that they were included in Paul's attacks on the Judaizers (Romans xi probably has the same purpose). It would be a full recognition of the fact that Jew and Gentile alike are fellow-heirs of the grace of life; they have 'communion in the Messiah', to quote a great Jewish Christian. We may feel that it is an olive-branch on the point of a bayonet; but it is a gesture of peace and reconciliation fitting the closing verses of such an Epistle.

The other translation is bolder, but Paul is quite capable of it. This is to take *kai* as 'even', 'that is to say', 'the equivalent of'. Linguistically, this is quite possible; the question must be solved theologically and exegetically. This would identify the new group, the 'third race of men' of whom the Church fathers delighted to talk—neither Jew nor Gentile, but Christian—with God's Israel. This is often put bluntly as 'the Church is the new Israel'. Put thus, we may well want to qualify the statement; but in broad outline, and as stated by Paul, it seems unexceptionable. In the first place, if *kai* does not mean 'even', then Paul is allowing two groups side by side in the kingdom of God; first, those who 'live according to the principle' enunciated in verse 15, and, secondly, God's Israel. But those of Israel who do not have this 'principle' are thereby automatically excluded from the true Israel, God's Israel. This is the inevitable deduction from Paul's reasoning above. In other words, while there is place for the believing Christian Jew in the kingdom, there is not for the Judaizer. Paul would go further. He would say that the 'believing Jew' belongs to Israel, but that the Judaizer does not. Thus there cannot be two groups; there can only be one. That was the battle Paul was fighting at Antioch, over 'table-fellowship' between Jewish and Gentile Christians.

Further, in passages like Colossians ii. 11 and (more strongly) Philippians iii. 2, 3, Paul seems to make the identification clear. Admittedly, the second is the famous controversial passage where he has already described the (unbelieving) Jews as 'dogs'—the term used by them to describe Gentiles. He has thus turned the tables. The (unbelieving) Jews are 'Gentile dogs'; they are 'mutilators' (*katatomēn*, not *peritomēn*); while the Christians are now 'the Jews' (*hē peritomē*). 'We', says Paul, 'are the Jews, we who serve God with spiritual worship, and make our boast of Christ, and do not trust in outward things.' It will be noted that many of the emphases here (*pneumati*, 'Spirit': *kauchōmenoi*, 'boasting': *sarki*, 'natural condition', 'outward circumstances') are also those of Galatians. But it is important to remember that, while Paul says that Christians are 'true Jews', he never says that Gentiles are Jews, nor Jews Gentiles; that is an illegitimate deduction. What he does say is that believing Jew and believing Gentile alike form the 'Israel of God', the instrument of His purpose. It is interesting to remember in the context of verse 16 that 'Peace upon Israel' is the great Old Testament blessing (Ps. cxxv. 5).

17. The *kopous parechetō*, 'make trouble for me' (NEB), is a phrase very common in the colloquial Greek of the papyri.

It is also freely used in the Gospels, as in Luke xi. 7 where one man 'knocks up' another man in the dead of night. In all such instances *kopous* has a bad sense, 'trouble', 'annoyance', 'bother'. Paul has used the corresponding verb *kopiaō* already in iv. 11 in the sense of 'labour', 'take pains'; there the sense is good. Indeed, in almost all his Epistles Paul uses this word of the 'toil' characteristic of, and inseparable from, the life of the true pastor. From such hard work Paul never asks to be freed; he has endured it gladly for this very Galatian church his one fear is that it may have all been in vain. What he does want to avoid is the endless harrying of the Judaizers, their endless insistence on *stigmata*, 'signs', borne *en tō sōmati*, 'outwardly'. To end all this persecution he will show them that he too bears 'distinguishing marks', but they are those that show him to belong to Jesus Christ, not to Jewry. It may be that the anxious queries of the wavering Galatians are also in his mind. He wants to set their hearts at rest too so that they may be able to give a similar reply when they are challenged.

We have already seen[1] the uses of *bastazō* in the Epistle. It always means 'to shoulder', 'to carry', with the idea that the object so moved is bulky and heavy. Therefore, whatever 'the marks of Christ' are, they are not to be borne easily. Further, Paul bears them *en sōmati*, 'bodily', 'outwardly'; therefore he cannot be referring simply to a spiritual state known only to himself.

But the heart of the problem lies in the question, What is the meaning of *ta stigmata tou Iēsou*, 'the marks of Jesus'? Later Christian theology, somewhat fancifully, interpreted this as meaning that marks appeared on Paul's hands, feet, and side, corresponding to Christ's wounds, so close was his identification with his Lord. The experience of certain mystics has been quoted as strictly parallel. Without going into the question of whether or no such physical manifestations have actually been reproduced in later days, and without inquiring into the means by which they may have been produced (which would seem to belong to the realm of abnormal

[1] See comments on v. 10 and vi. 2.

psychology), we may say that such an interpretation runs counter to all Paul's thought.

stigmata, in non-biblical Greek, is the word that is used to signify the 'marks', or 'brands' that distinguish a slave as belonging to a particular master, rather as cattle or sheep are 'branded' today. Such 'brands' are often mentioned in the 'placards' announcing the escape of runaway slaves, and many such documents have survived among the papyri. This is the most obvious meaning; and while the Jews do not seem to have had similar customs in Old Testament days, the practice of 'ear-marking' willing slaves is a close enough parallel (Ex. xxi. 6). The word *stigmata* is also freely used of 'ritual cicatrices' such as were common to many ancient and modern religions of the more 'primitive' type. Arndt-Gingrich suggest 'tattooing' as a modern parallel. If Paul is using the word in this sense, then he is deliberately classifying Jewish circumcision with these other gashes and marks. It is daring, but verse 12 (taken with Philippians iii. 2) shows that Paul was perfectly capable of such an identification. We could then paraphrase: 'You want me to bear ritual cuts and gashes, do you? I bear such scars already, but they are those that mark me out as Christ's man.'

So much for the interpretation, which is clearly that of NEB, 'I bear the marks of Jesus branded on my body'. But what are these brands? Almost certainly, since they are outwardly visible (*en tō sōmati*, 'in the body', involves this conclusion), they must be some of the scars borne by Paul as a result of his suffering for Christ's sake. Those who favour a South Galatian destination for the letter can point to the stoning at Lystra as a very relevant example (Acts xiv. 19), but 2 Corinthians shows us many other experiences which must have left scars. Stoning and flogging, whether by synagogue beadles or the dreaded Roman thongs, would leave unmistakable scars of suffering gladly endured for Christ's sake that marked out their bearer as Christ's man. Most of the relevant literature is quoted at the end of the excellent article in Arndt-Gingrich.

18. On this note of peace the Epistle will end, but, as his closing touch, Paul adds, as usual, 'The Grace'. We are more familiar with its use in the longer form of 2 Corinthians xiii. 14, 'The grace of the Lord Jesus Christ, and the love of God, and the fellowship of the Holy Spirit, be with you all'. This rich trinitarian formula is doubtless Paul's final development of the simple prayer that we have here: 'The grace of our Lord Jesus Christ be with your spirit, fellow-Christians.'[1] Yet we cannot say that the shorter form is less rich, though its richness may be less fully expressed. Rightly understood, all the fullness of the trinitarian 'Grace' is here too. Christ is here. He is central, as He should be in all expressions of the Christian faith.

He is *Jesus*, the 'Joshua' of the Old Testament, the 'saviour' of God. More, He is the *Christ*, the Anointed, the 'chosen One' of God's purpose, the fulfilment of all the hopes and aspirations of the Old Testament. His nature is fully expressed as *charis*, *grace*—the free undeserved love of God showered on man. We have said that Christ is grace personified; but He is more than that, for He is the very grace of God become incarnate. That is why we cannot speak of 'the grace of the Lord Jesus Christ' without at the same time referring to 'the love of God', whether we state it explicitly in so many words or not. For the Christian, in this shorter formula, this truth was safeguarded by calling Jesus *Lord*, the great title of God in Old Testament times. More, in many ancient witnesses, He is not only *kurios*, but *kuriou hēmōn, our Lord*; here is the peculiar sense of 'belongingness' that we have found to be characteristic of all Pauline thought. Lastly, this blessing is to be *meta tou pneumatos hūmōn, with your spirit*. For the Christian, in spite of the possibility of a purely general meaning, this can only recall the Holy Spirit, who is the

[1] A similar variety may be traced within the Bible in respect of baptismal formulae. The first disciples were only baptized 'into the name of the Lord Jesus' (Acts viii. 16), for that was all that was necessary for Jews who already had an intense belief in the one God, and who were already looking for the gift of the Spirit. Matthew xxviii. 19 gives the full 'trinitarian formula', doubtless very necessary in baptizing *ta ethnē*, 'the Gentiles', who had no such knowledge or expectations.

common bond of the common life, by whom alone we are *adelphoi*, 'full brothers' in Christ. To this prayer, with full meaning, Paul sets his 'Amen'.

NOTES

NOTES

NOTES

NOTES